MW00439855

Never Let 'Em See You Sweat

If you have to present to tough audiences, this book is a must. I've seen Phil Slott convince skeptical marketing managers to invest millions to produce his advertising and tens of millions to run it. He didn't sweat it. Take his advice and neither will you.

ALLEN ROSENSHINE
Chairman, CEO
BBDO Worldwide

At BBDO, Phil Slott was one of the masters of presentation. I worked side-by-side with him for close to ten years. And watching him present, I can honestly say, he could sell a disgruntled client with no budget and in a foul mood, a new, multi-million dollar campaign, and have the client thanking for the honor.

This book is a must read — not only for advertising people but for anyone who wants to improve their selling skills. It would be particularly useful for young people just coming into business.

I wish I had this book when I started out in.

PHIL DUSENBERRY
Chairman of the Board
BBDO, New York

Never
let 'em
see you sweat

A Tranquilizer For Presenters

Phil Slott

Ad-Land
P r e s s

ISBN 0-9679701-0-5

Library of Congress Control Number

00-132616

first edition

1 2 3 4 5 6 7 8 9 10

Text design by Bruce Taylor Hamilton

Front cover design by Phil Slott

First commercial

Dry Idea™ campaign

1986

Actor:

There are three nevers in Hollywood.

Never pick up the phone on the first ring.

Never say I'll be right over.

And never let 'em see you sweat.

To Mary:
I never sweated marrying you for a moment.

Contents

Never Skip This Introduction   1

Never Say Always   7

Never Confuse Public Speaking

    With Presentation   10

Never Be Pointless   24

Never Be Ignorable   33

Never Ignore The Other Guy   47

Never Drown In A Sea Of Faces   59

Never Let Their Agenda

    Be Your Agenda   69

Never Start Nervous   81

Never Trust One Rehearsal   91

**Never Believe They're Out
    To Get You**   104

Never Be Snowed   115

Never Forget Your Crutches   124

Never Run At The Mouth   136

Never Be Too Positive   146

Never Get Caught Lying   157

Never Be Arrogant   167

Never Be Too Serious   178

Never Stop Acting   189

Never Say Never   199

Never
Skip This
Introduction

If you skip this introduction, you won't know who I am or why I wrote this book. Here's the official version — a bio from my days in an advertising agency.

Phil's career began at Grey Advertising in 1964. Six years later, making stops along the way at other agencies such as McCann-Erickson; Foote, Cone & Belding; and J. Walter Thompson, he joined Ted Bates as a vice president, creative supervisor and was on his way to becoming a senior vice president and creative director.

Phil spent eight years at Ted Bates and went to Batten, Barton, Durstine and Osborn in 1978 as a senior creative director. The following year, he was elected a senior vice president and a member of the board. He was also named co-head of the new business committee.

In 1981, Phil became an executive vice president with BBDO. Before a move to London in 1985, he was second in command to Phil Dusenberry in BBDO Worldwide's highly-acclaimed creative department in New York City. In both cities, Slott was responsible for much of BBDO's growth with Gillette, one of the agency's largest multinational accounts.

In 1987, Phil became Chairman and Chief Creative Officer of Tracy-Locke. Based in Los Angeles, Phil had overall corporate responsibility for the agency's creative product.

Among many memorable campaigns Phil created and supervised over the years are TWA (*"Up, Up and Away"*), Arco (*"We Treat Your Car Like People"*), the US Navy (*"It's Not Just a Job, It's an Adventure"*), Caress Soap (*"Caress Before You Dress"*), Schweppes (*"The Tastemaker"*), Rondo (*"The Thirst Crusher"*), Campbell Chunky Soup (*"The Soup That Eats Like a Meal"*), and Dry Idea (*"Never Let 'Em See You Sweat"*). He has won numerous creative awards for these campaigns and others.

His Clios — the industry's highest honor — include Best Commercial and Best in Category. He has won the *Lion d'Or* and *Silver Lion* at the Cannes Film Festival and gold awards from the New York Art Directors Club and New York Copywriters Club. Three of his commercials are in the Museum of Modern Art's collection.

Phil Slott

Now, here's a more personal version of who I am.

I started out as a nervous junior copywriter in advertising. I used to pray on the floor of my apartment before simple meetings.

From there, as I became a calmer presenter, I went farther and farther up the corporate ladder.

Finally I was able to control my nervousness so well that I was comfortable making presentations to groups of all sizes, from a handful to a roomful. I was able to pitch a new razor campaign in front of hundreds of executives of Gillette Europe. And I was able to make dozens of multimedia presentations for my domestic company.

Presentation skills helped make me chairman of BBDO London and co-chair of Tracy-Locke.

I had to present constantly, and calm presentations are what got me up and out.

Advertising is the acid test of presenting, and I took this test for twenty-six years.

Ten years ago I wrote the slogan *"Never let 'em see you sweat!"* for Gillette's Dry Idea deodorant. This slogan and the "nevers" that go with it embody my philosophy about advertising:

Saying what you won't get is more compelling than saying what you will get.

When it comes to deodorants, saying *"Never let 'em see you sweat,"* was more compelling that saying "You'll always be dry." What proved to be compelling was what was avoided.

If you're still with me, here's why I wrote this book. First, I didn't write it to discuss content and this book doesn't address what you present.

This book does address how you present it.

What you say is up to you. How you say it is up to you and this book.

Phil Slott   **5**

Everybody has to present, but being a great presenter takes a lot more than a valium.

Great presenters may be born, but presenters can also be made great.

Few can change the talents they're born with, but anyone can change his approach. This book is designed to help you change your approach to presenting.

It's designed to help you be a great presenter by helping you be a calm presenter. In other words, it's designed as a tranquilizer.

Maybe you should read somebody else's book. Maybe.

Never
Say Always

Do not count your chickens before they are hatched.
Aesop's Fables

Never say always and the audience will never see you sweat.

A skilled presenter never takes props, aids, lighting, wardrobe or the podium for granted. This means you should never assume you know your script, charts, notes or your audience's attention span.

Never checking anything will keep your palms sweaty.

Never assuming anything will keep them dry.

One-on-one. One-on-two. One on twenty-two. One on twenty-two hundred. One on twenty-two thousand. One on twenty-two million.

Presentations come in all sizes: from your crew on the assembly line to the national sales force of IBM.

Presentations are given to all types of people: from senior citizens to Generation X.

Presentations are staged for every reason: from selling soft drinks to recruiting true believers.

Presentations are housed in many venues: from polished board rooms to sweaty locker rooms.

Presentations happen anywhere or anytime you're called on to be a showman. And the one thing that makes a successful presentation is not assuming anything.

Not assuming anything is only part of a successful approach. In the following chapters, each beginning with the word never, you'll pick up other tenets that I learned the hard way.

These are:

Never say always
Never confuse public speaking with presentation.
Never be pointless.
Never be ignorable.
Never ignore the other guy.
Never drown in a sea of faces.
Never let their agenda be your agenda.
Never start nervous.
Never trust one rehearsal.
Never believe they're out to get you.
Never be snowed.
Never forget your crutches.
Never run at the mouth.
Never be too positive.
Never get caught lying.
Never be arrogant.
Never be too serious.
Never stop acting.
Never say never.

Learning these "nevers" helped make me a great presenter. Now they can make you a great presenter too.

Phil Slott

Never
Confuse Public Speaking
With Presentation

Saying is one thing and doing is another.
Montaigne

Public speaking and presentation are not the same thing. Public speaking may be talking the talk, but presentation is *walking the walk*.

Public speaking is speaking well in public. Presentation is speaking well in public plus all the elements of showmanship.

Many would call Socrates, Abraham Lincoln, or George Will great presenters — but they're not. They were or are great public speakers.

In the business setting, presentations are a ray of light in most people's workday. People come to presentations to get away from the dull paper-work in their offices. They come to escape. They come for the show.

As a result, the presenter must always live up to the audience's expectations for entertainment. If you as a presenter don't do this, you will soon be labeled unsuccessful, and suffer the consequences that go with that label.

Skilled presentation involves acting, rehearsal, scenery, sound effects, and possibly music and lighting. A presentation may also call for the right make-up, hairstyle, props and an *apropos* wardrobe.

Public speaking only involves a few of these elements. Acting, rehearsal, timing and appearance are important to public speaking, but that's where the similarity ends.

Public speaking rarely involves cues, sound effects, scenery, music or lighting.

The challenge of presentation starts where public speaking leaves off.

Because presentation means "walking the walk," it's not surprising that some great presenters made their mark on history. So, who have been the greatest presenters in history? We could debate the answer to that question forever. But my own choices are Alexander the Great, Adolf Hitler and Carl Sagan.

Alexander, The Great

Did Alexander, the famed Macedonian conqueror, pay his men well? The record says yes. Did he feed his men well? Yes. Did he rotate his men well? Yes. Did he make sure his men heard from home? Yes. Was he a great public speaker? Sure.

But Alexander was a great presenter because he used showmanship and symbolism.

Alexander was the best showman on the battlefield. His men could see him because he was always on horseback and he always led from the front. He wore an outstanding uniform. He had polished armor, a flowing cape and sharp shiny weapons. In short, he was a great showman who showcased himself.

Alexander symbolized all the qualities his men felt a leader should stand for. They wanted him to be a symbol of bravery. He *was* brave, so his three-dimensional presence was inspiring. He was a living symbol.

His presence said "Look, here I am. I'm not

behind the lines eating grapes in some safe head-quarters. I'm out in front where it's life-threatening. I'm right here. They'll get *me* long before they get you."

He didn't communicate bravery by words. He communicated it through action. Alexander the Great was beloved because soldiers always love someone who walks the walk instead of just talking the talk.

Adolph Hitler

Adolph Hitler is deservedly maligned as an evil Fascist responsible for World War Two. In spite of that record, Hitler should be credited with being an excellent presenter.

I'm sure Goebbels taught him a few tricks, but Hitler also originated techniques of his own. He was a great presenter because he mastered both showmanship and symbolism.

His intuition for showmanship told him to begin his presentations with three minutes of absolute silence. Even in his speeches to audiences in the tens of thousands, he would begin with silence. Three whole minutes of silence! All he did was step up to the podium and stare at the audience for three long minutes.

Sound easy? Think you can do it? Try it.

More often, everybody wants to start talking right away, even if it's just to say: "Hey, I'm not going to say anything for three minutes."

The principle is that silence is a better attention-getting device than sound, and Hitler was able to confidently establish this silence better than anyone else, then or now.

When he finally began to speak, he began slowly and conversationally, in a matter-of-fact way. As he warmed up, he became patriotically emotional. He articulated the pain, embarrassment and nationalistic pride of the German people in the early twentieth century.

The Fuhrer's emotions were the people's emotions (well expressed in the phrase, *mein Fuhrer*) and he wasn't afraid to express them in public. Millions of people did his bidding because they saw him as one of them.

Hitler presented and staged a nationalistic spirit very forcefully. This included extensive and ingenious use of the German flag, the national anthem and German folk music. He employed Albert Speer, a brilliant and sympathetic architect, to help him design these presentations. Under his direction, Speer came up with the dramatic device of using columns of lights as an awesome prop, against a night sky, for a Hitler speech.

Presentation helped popularize Hitler. It helped the Germans regain their sense of pride. Unfortunately, it also misled the nation and helped them focus on war.

Carl Sagan

Hitler was the showman of the Third Reich, but Carl Sagan was the showman for a whole planet because he hoped to present life on earth to other galaxies and set about doing so.

Through the television series *Cosmos*, he was the first person to present the idea that we are "not alone" in the universe to an audience of millions.

Sagan was among the first to take the mystery of the universe out of the realm of science fiction, present it as tangible and popularize it.

He was the first person who actually developed symbols for life on earth and sent them into space on the Voyager spacecraft.

To do this he created a comprehensive message of earth-sounds designed to be received by extra-terrestrial beings elsewhere in the cosmos, a galactic greeting to be carried on a spaceship. The first "Hello, how are you?" designed for aliens.

This greeting was a true presentation. It included a disc that contained his sweetheart's heart-beat, samples of earth-music, samples of sixty different earth languages and a videotape of a typical earth-kiss.

Acting on his belief that "we are not alone" he conceived these ideal communications.

Sagan's best symbol was the idea of shooting the message off into space because he expected sentient life out there to receive it.

When Carl Sagan passed away in 1997, America not only lost an icon, the *earth* lost an icon.

Those are my nominations for three greatest presenters in history, but who are great presenters today? My choices come from the political arena. They are Elizabeth Dole and Bill Clinton.

Elizabeth Dole

Dole's performance at the Republican National Convention in 1996 is justly famous. It was a great presentation because she was able to combine showmanship and symbolism.

She presented while walking through the convention audience with a hand-held mike. She reached out and touched her listeners while she spoke, "Vote for my husband, the kind Republican."

Her sense of symbolism helped her present the Republican Party as friendly, informal and approachable. Dole found a fine way to translate the Republican message into a more sensitive feminine medium. Her sense of showmanship made sure the medium became the message.

Bill Clinton

Bill Clinton gave a good example of how presentation can save a career in 1998. He managed to bring off the his State of Union message in spite of being involved in a major White House sex scandal. He could do this because he's a great presenter. His presentation on the floor of

Congress was so masterly, he actually emerged without additional embarrassment.

Clinton is a master of symbolism and showmanship. His sense of timing is perfect and he's able to act as if he's speaking personally to each individual, even though the audience may number millions.

Making his point with his voice is just a start. He also makes it with the eyes, expressions and gestures. And he makes it with important symbols. For example, he reveals the passage of new minority programs in the setting of a minority neighborhood. Or, he reveals new ecological initiatives in ecological settings and invokes patriotism in patriotic settings. He even hired six former welfare recipients to work at the White House to symbolize the workfare program.

Clinton rarely signs a bill anywhere without

having a symbol standing by in person, a living symbol of what the problem is or who the bill will help.

He invites the disabled to the White House. He sees Boy Scouts and Girl Scouts in the field. He sees women in the military or out in the workplace. He helps blind people cross the street. And recently he invited disabled kids to the Rose Garden for the signing of the Education for the Disabled Bill.

He also presents the interests and leanings of his administration by appearing with actors, writers, artists and athletes.

If a material symbol like a wheelchair or a saxophone is suitable, then that's there instead of a person.

Whether he's acting or not, he seems to touch our hearts while he's touching our heads, and he appears to feel our pain as well as joy. If this is all role-playing, it's well played.

Public speaking is not the same as presentation. It's possible to be a great public speaker and a lousy presenter.

Presentation involves the talents of public speaking plus showmanship. Bill Clinton and Elizabeth Dole have this combination.

But the greatest presenters who ever lived were best at using showmanship and symbols. Alexander the Great was a great showman who himself symbolized bravery. Hitler used showmanship and symbolized German nationalism. And Carl Sagan used showmanship to symbolize that there might be other beings out there in the universe, ready to receive a symbolic message concerning Earth.

Phil Slott

Never
Be Pointless

"Today we're going to talk about coupon copy."

"Let's discuss what the Three Wise Men wore when they visited the manger."

"Shakespeare's diet doesn't get all the attention it should."

No, no, and no!

No one wants to hear presentations on these subjects because they're not important. They're pointless.

Pointlessness, not surprisingly, leads to mumbling, bumbling, fumbling and boredom. Pointlessness wastes time, money and effort.

Therefore, it is important to remember that the

single most important point in any presentation is having a point to make.

Have A Point

If you don't have a point to make, don't bother presenting.

Don't bother agonizing over the proposition.

Don't bother rehearsing its execution.

Don't bother with one-on-one research or focus groups.

You can set aside taste-tests, road-tests, fragrance-tests or in-home-use tests. Don't bother assigning speaking roles, picking a typeface or choosing a logo.

Having a point calms a presenter because having a point makes you an instant expert. This keeps you safe from hecklers who are generally afraid of experts, so they leave them alone.

Everybody pays attention to doctors, lawyers, pilots and architects because these guys are considered experts. But you don't have to have a graduate degree or a pilot's license to get the audience's attention. You just have to have your own key point.

This key point should be made first.

In the opening remarks, use slides, charts, sound effects or musical overture to emphasize the point. That way people know it's the most important point you are going to make.

That point should also be made last.

In the closing remarks use slides, charts, sound effects or musical climax, so people are sure that's what you want to leave them with.

Make your point first, last and frequently in between. Indeed, any point worth making is worth sticking to.

So, repeat it, return to it, say the same thing differently and never leave it.

In other words, be tenacious! Tenacious means focused and single-minded. Every presentation should be single-minded. Whether the point is made with slides, film, music, charts or by the statement of your own wardrobe, stick to it like glue.

Now that you have a key point, make sure it's tangible, relevant and simple.

Tangible

A tangible point is a nuts-and-bolts point. It's one you can take to the bank. It's where the rubber meets the road.

Decide what tangible goals you want to achieve before you present. If you don't have a reason as tangible as getting promoted, impressing the boss, winning new business, cutting expenses, signing them up, converting them, recruiting them or organizing the work force, don't present. If it won't increase the topline, decrease the bottom line or hold a fine line, don't bother presenting. If it's not as tangible as convenience, ease, efficacy or aesthetics, forget the whole thing.

Relevant

One man's meat is another man's poison. What's boring to most people most of the time, is important to some people some of the time.

The correct way to handle a grenade is only relevant if you're a soldier. Required reading is relevant when you're a student. Avoiding athlete's foot is particularly relevant for an athlete. Microchip technology is only relevant if you're in the computer field. The four life-saving steps are very relevant if you're going to need them because you do dangerous work.

No soldier has to know about flower arranging. No clergyman has to know much about "Fun City." And very few professors are asked to communicate in street-talk.

So, every point can't be relevant to every person, but some point is someone's stock in trade. It's vital to know the difference. That way you'll always be relevant when it counts.

Simple

Can you say it in a single sentence? Can you write on a matchbook? Can you make your point in the time it takes a traffic light to change.

We all forget complicated directions, and tend to remember simple ones. Think of any point you make as a presenter as directions you might be giving at a busy intersection. Think of the audience you present to as drivers who are trying to follow your directions.

All your successful points should be readily understood by the average person with an average IQ. Even rocket science, logarithms and brain chemistry can be grasped by the average high-school graduate if they're explained simply.

As you will rarely be presenting to doctors, professors or congressmen, keep that in mind. Complicated details should be reserved exclusively for an audience that understands complicated details.

Remember, every great idea, to be shared, had to begin with a simple presentation. Some caveman must have presented the wheel to another caveman.

Drive It Home

Now that you have a point and you know it's good, drive it home, put it in their faces and make sure it stays there. If you don't emphasize it, you've wasted the countless hours it took to get that point.

The only way to emphasize any point is to emphasize it selectively. It needs to stick out. Like the only rose in the desert. The only clap in an empty auditorium. Or the only whiff of smoke in the wilderness.

Emphasizing everything is really emphasizing nothing.

If your point is like a rose in a rose garden, a clap in a standing ovation, or smoke in a forest fire, your point will be lost.

The only point worth emphasizing is your main point, so never lose focus. Any point you don't emphasize is a minor point, on its way to becoming an invisible point.

In sum, a presenter should never bore any audience with a trivial presentation. Remember, you never deserve the audience's attention. You *win* it by having a point to make. And you keep their attention by having a good point to make.

Every successful presentation begins with a good point. Good points are tangible so they lead to meaningful results you can count on. Good points are relevant to members of the audience. And good points are simple enough to be understood by the average person who doesn't have time or inclination for a long lecture.

Once you have a good point, it's time to drive it home.

Never
Be Ignorable

Someone's boring me . . . I think it's me.
Dylan Thomas

What's the point of having a point if it's going to be ignored?

No presentation should ever be ignorable.

Here's my formula for ignorable presentations: Old + meaningless + forgettable = ignorable.

We've all sat through presentations that waste time. Presentations that could cure insomnia. Presentations that make us wonder if hearing it twice is last prize.

That's because the presenters have few new ideas. They're full of overly familiar thoughts and they're completely forgettable.

Too many Presidential speeches fall into this

category. Too many research presentations fall into this category, particularly those that bury one in data.

Too many marketing presentations fall into this category, particularly marketing presentations that swamp one with product specifications.

We've all been harangued by ignorable car salesmen, insurance salesmen and telemarketers. We've all watched our secondhand click around the watch. We've all gotten sore butts and bleary eyes. We've all been made overtired and over-heated. We've been over-dosed, over-charted and under-engaged.

But there's no reason why you should cause an audience to doodle or turn drowsy or, worse, fall asleep.

Never say anything old and tired. Never say

anything meaningless. Always say something memorable, and keep your goals in sight.

If you give an ignorable presentation, it deserves to be ignored.

Here's my formula for presentations that can't be ignored:

New + meaningful + memorable = unignorable.

New

New can mean a look at an old problem from a new perspective. It can be an idea that demands change, an extension of something old, or a completely new idea.

Some advertising campaigns were new because they pushed for changes in lifestyle, radical shifts in attitude or changes in behavior.

When Volkswagen introduced "think small," they weren't only selling cars, they were asking people to change their lifestyles. A change from low mileage, cushy cars that let the rider stretch out in comfort, to high-mileage, Spartan cars that made people cramp-up in discomfort. There were jokes about how many people could fit in a Volkswagen. Whoever presented this new idea must have shocked his first audience.

Another surprising lifestyle idea was presented to the folks at Honda Motorcycle. "You meet the nicest people on a Honda" must have been a shocking advertising line in the Sixties when the bikes were ridden primarily by Hell's Angels.

My advertising agency won the Jacqueline Cochran perfume account by telling the client that perfume isn't bought with the nose, it's bought with the eyes! We said that optic nerves are more important than olfactory nerves, imagery is more important than odor. At that time, that idea was shocking to those in the fragrance business.

The idea that Miller Lite Beer could be "less filling and taste great" must have been shocking initially because most people assumed beer had to be filling *and* full of calories to taste good.

An L.A. agency once recommended that Taco Bell pursue single males because single males ate most of the Mexican food Taco Bell sold and comprised most of their business. This was an uncomfortable idea at first because McDonalds, the fast-food industry leader, catered to families. Yet the ad agency was proven right.

Other lifestyle presentations that once had to pass the "new" test took place at Apple Computer, Nike Shoes and Sony.

Phil Slott

Some marketing strategies have passed the "new" test, too.

Like McDonalds' "finger food" and Japanese luxury goods.

Well-mannered people used to eat with silverware. Picking food up with your hands was a shocking — and bright — new idea.

Similarly, Japan long had a reputation for making cheap toys and gadgets out of US beer cans. But it's a long way from a tin car to a Lexus.

The idea that "It's a Sony!" meant something good was a shocking idea and made a shocking presentation.

There are non-advertising examples of new ideas as well. When Frank Lloyd Wright presented his all-glass house, it must have seemed a shocking trade-off between architectural beauty and loss of privacy.

Other examples include: the glue that didn't stick well but turned out to be perfect for the Post-It; a system of fastening modeled after a weed that turned into a consumer product called Velcro; and the idea that the Internet could bring a world of information into a person's home. All of these probably made startling presentations when first introduced.

The New Test

To make sure you've got a new idea, give the presentation the "new" test. This test has two simple questions. The answers will reveal if your idea has ever been heard before. Is the audience still calm? (A "no" answer means you've flunked.) Is the audience shocked? (A "yes" answer means you've passed and you're on your way to making an unignorable presentation.)

Meaningful

Meaningful means a presentation with tangible, tactile goals. The goals could be yours, like selling something, trying to win friends or getting promoted. Or the goals could be the audience's, like choosing the right product or promoting the right candidate.

Controversial combinations can make presentations meaningful. Confronting an audience that strongly supports a position with a presentation on the opposing point of view can make the presentation especially meaningful.

Michael Crichton in his book *Travels* crafted a controversial presentation for the Committee for the Scientific Investigation of Claims of the Paranormal. He supported the existence of paranormal phenomena and was able to present an argument that had the publishers of *The Skeptic*

nodding their heads in agreement. Taking a controversial position with a tough audience pushes
you to think like the opposition and create a
thoughtful, meaningful presentation.

Other examples of controversial combinations
include: Presenting on the right-to-life at a NOW
meeting. Presenting on doctor-assisted suicide to
the Christian Coalition. Presentations to service-
women against women in combat. A presentation to gays about "Don't ask, don't tell."
Presentations on smoker's rights to new mothers.
Presentations on property rights to environmentalists.

The Meaningful Test

This test is simple but necessary: Were the goals
tangible and were they achieved?

Are more feminists avoiding abortion? Are

more believers allowing doctors to assist their terminally ill family members to die? Are fewer service women applying for combat branches? Are more gays more comfortable in the military? Do more new mothers appreciate smoking sections? Are more environmentalists considering the rights of property owners as well as the needs of the ecosystem?

Whether you agree with your results or not, if you want to make an unignorable presentation, they better be tangible!

Memorable

Memorable generally means new plus meaningful. If you've heard it before, or it's not important, it goes in one ear and out the other. If it's new and meaningful, it stays inside.

You can use memory hooks to be doubly sure

that your message gets through and really sticks.

Memory hooks might paraphrase something familiar. For example, "To go, or not to go, that is the question."

Or use rhyme. "It's never too late for Caltrate."

Memory hooks could derive from a well-known quote: "The only thing we have to fear, is fear itself."

Or use humor. The audience will remember, "He's the guy who told the one about the three New Yorkers."

Or use famous music. For example, Joy perfume was remembered after they used the song "April in Paris," in a commercial.

Other Memory Hooks Include:

Behaving oddly: "I can't forget that guy. He stood on his head."

Using different props: "She wore a snake."

Having someone come up from the crowd to demonstrate: "He called Bill up on stage to hold the hat."

Imitating someone. "I never knew he could imitate Bogey."

Using distinctive body language. Standing up at the right time, banging your fist, clapping your hands, pointing or falling down like Buster Keaton are all memory hooks.

The Memorable Test

The memorable test is simple — does the audience remember it one day later, two days later, a week later? Are sales going up? Are uniforms worn correctly? Are they considering the opposite point of view?

Do they remember the memory hook itself?

Making your presentation memorable means that you will have the opportunity to impact the audience's attitudes, ideas, and possibly even behavior long after the presentation is done.

Is it new? Is it meaningful? Does the audience remember it? If the answer to all these questions is "yes," you have an unignorable presentation.

History proves this. When JFK said, "Ask not what your country can do for you, ask what you can do for your country."

Or when he said: "The torch has been passed."

When Douglas MacArthur promised, "I shall return."

Or when Dr. Martin Luther King said, "I have a dream."

These were all new, meaningful and memorable ways to say, variously, pitch-in for America, I am the President now, I'll be back, and here is my vision. There are countless other historical examples from Abraham Lincoln's Gettysburg Address to Mayor Fiorello La Guardia's reading of the funny papers on radio. From Winston Churchill's wartime speeches to his famous British after-dinner toasts.

These statements all add up to the same thing: They were all new, all meaningful, and they're all memorable.

Never
Ignore The Other Guy

Members of the audience must be respected.
Laurence Olivier

Ignoring the other guy means losing touch with him. It means being all about you instead of being all about the audience.

Alexander the Great, Hitler and Martin Luther King did not ignore the other guy. Because of this, their abilities to identify and motivate are now legendary.

Alexander the Great's soldiers wouldn't have fought for him if he ignored them. Hitler's SS never would have committed mass murder without his motivation. And Martin Luther King's followers never would have protested if he hadn't reached out and touched them, heart and soul.

The same goes for preachers and cult leaders.

If preachers ever ignored the other guy, they would never inspire their congregations. Their congregations wouldn't pray, sing or clap with them either.

If cult leaders ignored the other guy, their followers wouldn't believe in other planes of existence or commit mass suicide.

You can't ignore the other guy when you're presenting either. That kind of egotism will lead you to confusion.

You'll confuse the audience's disapproval with their approval. You might mistake their shock for enthusiasm. You could confuse sarcasm with endorsement. You could interpret shaking heads as nodding heads. You will think their outrage is only embarrassment.

Most bad presenters are on send instead of on receive. This means their presentations will be costly and ineffective.

You pay a big price for ignoring the other guy. Three examples of what can happen, besides confusion, are presentations that lose sales, presentations that lose votes and presentations that cost lives.

Ignore The Car Buyer, Lose The Sale

Let's say the customer looks like a yuppie — young, athletic and sporty. So you throw a sales pitch that sells a hot sports car with great pick-up and tight cornering.

But it happens that looks are deceiving this time. Turns out the customer is totally safety conscious — a driver who wants rapid-response air bags more than aerodynamic design. An alternate braking system more than a constant accelerating system. And side-impact standards more than a spoiler.

If you'd taken an interest in this buyer's habits and asked personal questions, if you'd gotten to know this customer first, you could have tailored the pitch and made the sale.

Instead, you too quickly accepted a stereotype. You ignored the buyer and lost the sale.

Ignore Volunteers, Lose Votes

Volunteers are not an honor-bound, dedicated work force that you can take for granted. Volunteers aren't any kind of stereotype. They are individuals. If you want their best effort in getting out the vote, for example, you need to appreciate them as people.

When you present to unpaid volunteers, do so

from a sincere understanding of their goals and challenges. You'll want to motivate, inspire and enthuse them.

Most of all, volunteers expect to be thanked. Part of your presentation had better thank them, very sincerely, from the bottom of your heart.

If you take their effort for granted and ignore their feelings, they won't help get the vote out.

Ignore Nurses, Risk Patients

Presenting to nurses is one example of presenting to an audience of professionals. So, why do extra work to motivate these paid professionals?

Simple. If nurses don't go that extra mile, the patient may die. Nurses are paid to do the job, but they're not paid for the extra mile.

They'll go the extra mile if and when they're inspired to.

Phil Slott   **51**

Your job as a presenter to health care workers is to go beyond any "hospital worker" stereotype and lend them that very inspiration.

Ignoring nurses, by not getting to know them, might actually cost a human life!

The way to make a car sale is by getting to know the buyer. The way to get out the vote is to care about the volunteers. The way to really save patients is to empathize with their nurses.

But how do you get to know them when you're behind a podium, they're shrouded in darkness and you only have an hour together? Here are some ways to get to know your audience.

Do Your Homework

You can learn a lot about an audience before you present to them, but you have to do your homework. Find out about the demographics of the group, their work habits and future hopes. And if members of your audience are members of an organization, know as much as you can about the organization in advance.

Work The Crowd

There's much you can learn from idle conversation. Take advantage of this by shaking hands, milling around and chatting with the audience before you begin.

What Are They Wearing?

Wardrobe can be very revealing. It reveals important things like attitudes, opinions, professions and politics.

Blue suits say one thing, sports clothes say another. And printed dresses may say a third thing. What people wear tells you who they are.

Presenters have an opportunity to observe what the audience is wearing outside, on the way in, and through out the presentation. You can use all of these opportunities.

When you understand your audience, you can adjust your presentation to please them, motivate them or influence them.

Consider The Questions Asked

Questions like these are really answers: "Do most women really want the right to choose?" "Does smoking guarantee you'll get lung cancer?' "Are you for states' rights, or should the federal government decide on everything?"

You can't always know a lot about an audience before a presentation, but if you had paid close attention to questions like these, you'd have learned a great deal.

You'd learn that you're presenting to a right-to-life audience. You'd intuit that you're presenting to a pro-tobacco audience. And you'd know you're presenting to a group of conservatives.

These questions reveal the kinds of attitudes and opinions that you can use to adjust your pitch right in midstream. It's never too late to modify a presentation to reach your desired goal.

Consider Their Body Language

Heads up, heads down. Heads in one hand, heads in both hands. Glassy eyes, focused eyes. Rolling eyes, squinting eyes. Loud applause, faint applause. Deep laughter, superficial laughter. Pointing fingers, twiddling thumbs.

Body language can send revealing signals and if you're not ignoring these signals you can learn a lot.

Let's take their opinions, attitudes or state of mind — like whether they appear to agree or disagree, whether they're bored or interested. Convinced or unconvinced. Like you personally or don't.

Reading body language is a great way to read an audience. Body language can tell you many things you want to know without the audience uttering a single phrase.

God Is In The Details

As architect Mies van der Rohe used to say, "God is in the details." Success with the other guy is also in the details.

Details like where he went to school, what

branch of the military he served in, or what his political views, attitudes, opinions or religion might be.

Details can also win friends. Like saying *semper fi* if they're Marines or talking about the break at Pipeline if they're surfers. Details like saying *ca va?* if they're French or *Guten tag* if they're German.

A most pleasing way to recognize the other guy is in his own language. JFK is famous for having done just that when he said *"Ich bin ein Berliner"* during the Berlin Wall crisis in Germany. The crowd went wild.

Knowing details about the other guy can mean getting an agreement early on. "Get 'em nodding" as we used to say in advertising. "Laughing on line" as they say in the theater.

Understanding the other guy can also make

early allies. Early allies make you more comfortable all the way through.

An audience can either play defense for you by nodding, laughing, crying, applauding and voicing approval.

Or they can play offense against you by blocking, jeering and running interference. It's up to you.

Nothing can make a presenter more nervous than ignoring the other guy. And nothing can make you calmer than knowing the other guy in advance.

Never
Drown In A Sea Of Faces

The human brain starts working the moment you are
born and never stops until you stand up
to speak in public.
Sir George Jessen

If you see your audience as a sea of faces, they'll become a sea of faces for sure. If you feel like you're presenting to a crowd, it's only a matter of time before the audience becomes a crowd.

The first signs of drowning are when all the faces run together into one huge face, a huge face that stops looking and starts staring.

Next, the sounds run together into one continuous sound. The tone in the room goes from recognizable words to an audible, nerve-wracking hum. All too suddenly, the audience is as contentious as the British House of Commons.

Then they stop pulling for you and start pushing against you. They start competing. They start snickering, jeering, heckling and trying to make you look bad.

The last and final sign of drowning is your own nervousness. Nervousness that causes confusion, stammering and more nervousness.

One example of drowning in a sea of faces happened at Tracy-Locke when we tried, and failed, to save the Taco Bell account.

In that case, the body language of the Taco Bell audience was so negative and scary, they became a crowd no matter *what* we did, or how many of them there really were.

They were rude. They looked at their watches, looked at the floor, read files, passed notes back and forth, and talked to each other. They cared more about themselves than did about us. They tested us by asking questions they already knew the answers to, and tried to sink the ship by seeing if we'd make a mistake.

They made us nervous. And we had a hard time not drowning. Fact is, everybody drowns in a sea of faces sometimes, but there are ways to stay afloat.

How To Stay Afloat

You can stay afloat if you transform the audience from a sea of faces you drown in, to a pond full of friends you can swim with.

Find Simpatico Faces

A crowd can often be a real crowd, but a few *unsimpatico* people can make a few people seem like a crowd in your mind.

The best way to deal with any crowd is to pick out people you like and who like you, and then focus and present exclusively to them.

If you present to *simpatico* people, you can't drown in a sea of faces because you're floating in calm water.

The most *simpatico* quality to look for is a sense of humor. That means folks who laugh at the right times and don't laugh at the wrong times. Then there are more subtle qualities like an attitude that matches your own, basic agreement with your point of view and a familiar appearance.

I was lucky to be able to present to several *simpatico* clients at the Gillette Company. Those guys okayed my campaigns, allowed me to produce them and made me feel part of the Gillette family. As a result, I gave some of my best presentations to Gillette and I will always think of them fondly.

Treat The Audience As Friends And Equals

Whether they're young or old, black or white, male or female, whether they're junior or senior, experts or beginners, it's important to treat them all like equals. This is no time to be superior, elitist or prejudiced.

Present as if you were all members of the same family. As if you were addressing our problem, not your problem or their problem.

Make Eye Contact With One Warm Face

Once when I had to present to hundreds of blue Navy uniforms, it would have been easy to panic. I would have panicked except that the Admiral himself kept me above water. He supplied that one warm face.

I was trying to convince the Navy to adopt the advertising campaign slogan, "It's Not Just a Job, It's An Adventure." I saw a sea of faces. I almost drowned in endless waves of blue and gold. The blur of uniforms made me dizzy. Hundreds of mumbling voices created a dull distraction. But focusing on the Admiral kept me afloat.

Thanks Admiral!

Present To Someone Your Own Age

Once when we were pitching a computer account in Dallas, I was able to stay afloat because the head of the company was in his thirties, like me. He was also a friendly man. He was the company president, and he and I locked eyes frequently, because we had youth in common.

It's also possible to focus on someone with whom you have maturity in common. In this case you may have gray hair, wisdom, experience and an easygoing approach that's shared. If so, why not use it?

Take The Inside Track

Being an insider will keep you from drowning. As one example, at one time I was able to convince the Jacqueline Cochrane Company to give their business to our agency because I was able to behave like an insider.

Jacqueline Cochrane makes L'Air du Temps perfume for women and Pierre Cardin cologne for men.

I became an insider by learning their business and getting together with staffers frequently before the presentation. At the presentation itself, I was able to offer some decent insights about the fragrance business.

Since the fragrance business has traditionally been run by women, it was hard as a male to become an insider. But, apparently I did, because we got the account.

Let's Get Physical

Nothing makes you as familiar with your audience or your audience as familiar with you, as getting physical.

It's helpful to walk and talk your way through the aisles before you present. You can shake hands, tell jokes, ask questions, gossip and chat with people on the way to the podium.

Presidents and congressmen usually do this. Attend a political function and you can see it in action.

This is an old campaign tactic for very good

reasons. It gets votes! It not only warms up the voters, it warms up the candidates and it warms the cause.

Oprah Winfrey's TV talk show is another example of getting physical. She walks casually through the audience talking and sometimes sitting. She talks to people one-on-one. And she's not afraid to reach out and touch a person every now and then. She gets to know her audience so well, she's able to joke with them and share their deepest secrets.

Many other presenters get physical. Singers often sit on the edge of the stage or sing in the aisles. Magicians will ask for volunteers. Dancers call for partners. And comedians ask for unwitting straight men.

This tactic will help you as a presenter too. Ask people up on stage to assist with demonstrations.

Pose questions. Make them shout out their answers. You can get people to come forward as examples of their height, taste, intelligence, even suits or shoes. You can get their opinions or get them to give a high five.

There's rarely a way to give a great presentation without getting physical. As the Chinese used to say, telling is good. Showing is better. Doing is the best.

If you perceive a sea of unfriendly faces, that's exactly what you'll get. You'll end up by drowning in that sea. But if you can personalize the audience, befriend them, find something in common and get physical, you'll stay afloat.

It's true that what you see is what you get. You'll drown in what you see if you don't turn the Wild Bunch into the Brady Bunch.

Never
Let Their Agenda
Be Your Agenda

I may have MS, but it doesn't have me.
Joseph Hartzler, Denver Federal Prosecutor

Most presenters let the audience's agenda become their agenda. That's because most audiences try to take over the agenda. They're know-it-alls who believe they're experts at everything you want to communicate. And they believe making you squirm proves it.

But there are ways to control the agenda by not being surprised. And there are ways to control the agenda by owning it.

Surprising You Is The Way They Control The Agenda

The best surprise is no surprise. But there's a lot

you can do when it happens. You can be surprised, be prepared and retain control at the same time. Consider that you can be:

Surprised By Your Competition

Sharks are circling right inside your own company. Sharks that will kill for your job, a similar job or a more senior job.

Sharks are also circling right outside your own company. Sharks who would kill to be the number one brand. Sharks who would kill to be first in the marketplace. Sharks who just want to have a better product than yours.

In a presentation setting, these sharks attack by surprise. They may try to make you stammer and look bad. They want you to misspeak, misquote or make costly errors. Surprise could mean that your equipment fails, so you'll fail.

If you accept that the competition will win

when you fail, you're off to a good start. It pays to prepare from this mind set.

There is no reason for these competitive sharks to surprise you or for them to end up costing you.

Surprised By Being Jeered

It doesn't matter how many presentations you've made or how smooth you've gotten at making them, being suddenly and unexpectedly jeered by an audience is still a shock.

But don't let them victimize you. You can be ready by rehearsing your response.

The best way of handling jeers is to make a joke about them. Treat them lightly by saying things like, "I never liked that idea either, how about this one?" Or, "I knew I should have stayed in bed this morning."

Once you get them laughing, the crisis is over and the agenda is yours again.

Surprised By Short Notice

Suppose someone says, "Ed, when we get inside, tell us what you know about cold fusion."

Bingo! You're surprised by short notice. It happens all the time because most people don't appreciate how long it takes to create an "off-the-cuff" presentation.

As Mark Twain said, "It usually takes me more than three weeks to prepare a good impromptu speech."

One way to look impromptu, even though you're not, is to be prepared by creating a list of relevant topics you are ready to present.

In network interviews, no matter what question they are asked, professionals always respond with what they've prepared. No matter what the question is, respondents always answer with the same pre-rehearsed statement.

When I was in England, I was frequently expected to give long after-dinner toasts. I solved this problem by preparing, memorizing and rehearsing some relevant topics. This way, I was never surprised by suddenly having to be the toastmaster.

Preparation can rescue you from many impromptu occasions. So can reduced expectations.

Reduce your expectations about the amount of time you usually devote to preparing a presentation. Short notice can become enough notice if you assume you may not get any notice.

With a shorter wind-up and constant preparation, short notice isn't surprising, it's expected.

Surprised By Difficult Questions

There's no way to always have the answer for every question asked. But you can do your best.

I used to do a group rehearsal with the participants before any big meeting. We'd get together and do a mock drill of sample questions and answers, such as:

"If they ask about scheduling, let Ed answer it."

"If they ask how much, nobody should answer it."

"If they ask about distribution, I'll take it."

Everybody hated doing this, but it always saved our agenda.

Surprised By Being Surprised

The best way to avoid surprise is to expect it. Presenters should just count on it. That way they can rehearse the jokes, the responses and the body language that put them back in charge of the agenda.

The best surprise may be no surprise. But next

best is not being surprised by the unexpected.

BOO! Hopefully, I didn't getcha.

Ownership Is The Way You Control The Agenda

In rock climbing, the rock has to be on your agenda. If you were on the rock's agenda, you'll fall for sure.

In surfing, the wave has to be on your agenda. If the wave's in charge, you'll wipeout.

In the martial arts, if the opponent's on your agenda you'll win. If you're on his agenda, you'll lose.

If you're on the audience's agenda, it probably means they'll see you sweat for sure.

It's got to be *your* agenda. If it is, you won't fall, wipeout or lose and they won't see you sweat!

Here are some ways to own the agenda:

Have An Owner's Body Language

Enter like you own the place. Move like you own the place. Answer questions like you own the place. Exit like you own the place. Never act sheepish, insecure or wimpy.

It's your presentation. You conceived it, you created it. You're going to take full responsibility for the contents. And you're going to take full responsibility for the delivery.

Never, never act like the audience owns the place.

Take The First Or Last Position

Audiences sag in the middle. They're at their most attentive at the beginning and end. Therefore, if you have the first and last words, you'll probably give the most memorable presentation of the day.

Look Good, Feel Good

You may be most relaxed in a dark power suit, blue jeans or a slinky dress. You may be happiest in black, white or bright colors. You may like your hair up, down, long or short. You may be more confident if it's parted. Or more confident if it's worn in bangs.

The important goal is to feel confident. Looking good means appearing the way you feel most comfortable, and therefore you're most confident.

Be Controversial

Never be afraid to be shocking. You should search for more ways to be outrageous. You're in control when you're shocking, different and outlandish.

The audience is reacting to you. You're not reacting to the audience.

Tell Intimate Stories

Vice-President Gore told the Democratic National Convention an emotionally charged account of losing his sister to cancer. As a result, he became more appealing because he became more human. As a result, it became his agenda.

Be The Moderator

When you're the moderator, it's your agenda. People are more concerned with working on the agenda than working on you.

Ask for their help, call on them, ask questions at random, ask scheduled questions, ask for help with demonstrations or ask them to read pieces aloud.

All this planning ensures you've got the control that's due a moderator.

Take charge! Working from your own agenda really works.

You're a lot less nervous when you're speaking for your own reasons — reasons like earning a promotion, getting a transfer, making a sale or winning an account. You're not an underling who speaks at someone else's behest. The agenda belongs to you! And when it's your's, they never see you sweat.

Have I (pronounced ee)

I is the Chinese word for will power.

Will power is a precious commodity. It means direction, desire, purpose and command. The Chinese treat *I*, and those who have it, with a great deal of respect.

Athletes can feel their opponent's *I* when they take the field, the gym floor or the court.

A boxer can feel his opponent's *I* before the first punch is thrown. Pitchers and hitters can feel each other's *I* sixty feet away.

Presenters also need *I*.

When you have *I*, there's no doubt that you're the boss, you're in charge, and it's your agenda.

The audience can tell you have a commanding presence even before the lights go out. They know you're in charge and they're not.

So, we're not all born with the massive *I* of G. Gordon Liddy, Clint Eastwood or Toshiro Mifune. The next best thing presenters can do is have the confidence that they have an important point to make. Confidence equals *I*.

Bottom line — never be surprised, always control the agenda, make sure you own the agenda, and cultivate *I*.

If you do these things, they'll never see you sweat.

Never
Start Nervous

Start out how you mean to finish.
English adage

Everybody knows you have to concentrate on a presentation while you're giving it. But few people realize you have to concentrate on a presentation before you give it.

It's important to start calmly. If you start nervously, you'll present nervously.

Here are some tricks that kept me from making that mistake.

Avoid Last-Minute Stress

Don't take on big challenges that cause excitement, anxiety, conflict or worry when you're getting ready to make a presentation. This not only takes your mind off the job at hand, it adds to your anxiety. Nothing makes you sweat more than presenting after an argument.

Punch The Heavy Bag

It's much better to take your frustrations out on a punching bag than it is to take them out on an audience. And there are always frustrations with any presentation.

Everybody gets frustrated when they have to think of what to say, write what they have to say, or worry about saying what they have to say.

It really helps to spend some time hitting something like a heavy bag.

I studied karate for years because it was better to hit a student in the first row of class than it was to hit someone in the first row of a meeting.

Enter With Gusto

Come in jauntily. Take long strides. Think of yourself as a pitcher walking to the mound or a tennis player taking home court. Or a quarter-back taking the field at a home game.

After all, you know your presentation is well conceived. You know it's well planned. And you know you're going to give it well.

It fills the hole in your soul, and puts some slip in your hip, if you look and feel athletic.

Check 'em once and check 'em twice

Checking over your notes one last time builds confidence and destroys the jitters.

It's like straightening a dress or tie. It's like a last check of your make-up before you go on stage, or checking a gun before you go on guard duty.

You've already done the hard work — this is just to help you relax.

Dress Well

Many performers know that they have more

confidence when they wear certain colors. Some apprehensive singers and comedians feel they perform better when they wear dark colors. And, of course, Johnny Cash only wears black.

Trial and error can tell you what colors produce your best presentation. You already know you present well. Dressing well has the same value as checking your notes.

Turn Nervousness Into Excitement

Technically speaking, the brain is unable to distinguish excitement from fear. Feeling jazzed-up feels the same, biologically, whether you are nervous or frightened.

So why not put this to good use by turning fear into excitement? You might feel afraid, but as far as your brain is concerned you're just excited.

Turning your nervousness into excitement is

like putting on a "game face" before a ball game. It keeps you calm to get up for a presentation the same way the real ballplayer gets "up" for a game.

It can be calming to feel aggressive. Being aggressive builds confidence, and confidence fights nervousness. Coaches and players know this. And presenters should know it.

If you don't channel your nervousness into excitement, that raw energy is going to waste!

Focus On Results

Start by focusing single-mindedly on winning the game, whatever your game may be.

To start by focusing on results will keep you from getting nervous, by keeping you goal-oriented.

You can't start nervous when you know the

best way to start, what you want to achieve and where you're going to finish. It keeps you calm to have a game plan.

There are lots of things you can do regularly long before you take the stage:

Be Healthy

You have to be healthy before you present, if you want to stay calm while you present.

Diet, health and fitness have always been my hobby because they have always kept me calm in a high-pressure racket.

I was the only one in my advertising agency who worked at triathlons — because triathlons worked for me.

I was the only member of the board who refused to drink alcohol or eat meat at board luncheons because I was the only member of the board who was a vegetarian. Lighter food leaves me with more energy to present.

Sound sleep, good nutrition and a balanced diet that was low on coffee and sugar, really did work for me.

Of course, I skipped booze, grass, coke and drugs because they cause confusion.

Techniques which I learned from alternative medicine like a relaxing herb, acupuncture and body work were effective, too.

They say there'd be no long distance bicycle race like the Tour de France if the competitors weren't given massages each day.

And in the world of presentation, I found that a massage helped before presentations. It's a good thing that massage is available in towns and hotels all over the world. They always made for a better presentation.

Phil Slott

These days there are also gadgets from pillows to foot rollers, virtual-reality videos to stretching aids, tapes, hot packs and cold eye shades to help you relax.

The choices are bewildering but useful. You should use whatever works.

Stay In Shape

Exercise also produces tangible results.

Running, swimming, weight-lifting and countless triathlons kept me calm before hundreds of presentations. Exercise gets rid of stress by giving it a place to go. Keeping in good shape will keep your presentations in good shape.

Loose-As-A-Goose

I not only kept in shape every day, I kept loose every day. Stretching keeps you loose as a goose. And, we all know what honking good presenters geese are!

Yoga is only one way to stretch. Others stretches come from team sports, the military, aerobics and countless other classes.

Dynamic Tension

Since a lot of presentations are given on the road, you'll need a portable way to stay healthy and relaxed.

Both dynamic tension and yoga allow for this. You only need your own body. And you have it when you catch planes, trains and buses. You bring it to hotel rooms, restaurants, theaters, offices and meetings. So why not use it?

Meditate

There's a whole spectrum of meditative techniques to choose from, and they all help make you calmer when you present. You can choose among Zen (my choice), transcendental meditation, yogic meditation, and many others.

There are also dozens of calming techniques you can learn, try out and use before you start.

The basic objective behind them all is to replace the use of the cognitive mind with what comes naturally. In other words, to become more intuitive. Sometimes your mind gets in the way.

Pray

Who knows, God may have just enough time between meetings to calm you down.

Never letting 'em see you sweat in a presentation is easy. All you have to do is start calmly.

Never
Trust One Rehearsal

When you are not practicing, remember, someone
somewhere is practicing, and when you meet him,
he will win.
Senator Bill Bradley, ex-New York Knicks player

One rehearsal doesn't do the job. One rehearsal only gets you ready for the second rehearsal.

If you don't rehearse a lot, you'll end up nervous, tongue-tied and embarrassed. You could mispronounce words and say things twice.

You could forget important points or remember unimportant points. You'll forget your lines. You might turn red. Then you'll get more nervous because you forgot your lines and turned red.

You will not achieve your goals.

You will not promote anything including yourself. You will not elect a mayor or get yourself elected. You will not increase sales or make yourself salesman of the year.

If lots of rehearsals mean you end up memorizing your part, so much the better. When you've memorized your part, you can give it in your sleep, under combat or under stress. You look casual and feel casual, because you are casual.

Rehearse Instead Of Deny

You have to accept that you are going to present before you can do it well. You can't pretend it's not going to happen like an alcoholic pretending he's not going to have a drink. Or wake up the morning of the presentation and plan to do it off the cuff.

Most people practice denial when it comes to presentation. They don't even want to think about it until they're up on stage.

They haven't rehearsed because rehearsal itself

forces them to face the fact that they are going to present. But the fact is, these people should know that rehearsal equals casual.

Rehearse In Front Of A Mirror

Why look blasé and drift off, if you're presenting on nuclear war? Why look intense if you're talking about business as usual?

You must appear to have a thorough command of the subject. They won't buy anything from you if you don't seem to understand what you're talking about.

Expressions are a basic part of any presentation. So practice smiling, frowning, glowering and laughing in front of a mirror.

If you don't, you could end up with counterproductive facial expressions or body language that conveys the opposite of what you want to say.

Check on your expressions and body language before it's too late.

Rehearse Out Loud

Mulling over a speech in your mind does not substitute for voicing it out loud.

Visualizing does help, but it does not qualify as a full rehearsal. Visualizing works so well, you can think you've given a presentation when you really haven't. Visualizing, instead of actually voicing the words, can result in mixed-up sentences, mispronounced foreign names and malapropisms.

You can't just mull it over; you simply have to say the things out loud.

Rehearse In Front Of Your Spouse

He or she is very handy, so, why not put dinnertime, drive-time or TV time to good use?

Instead of criticizing, gossiping or arguing, why not use your spouse to assess the presentation and help you rehearse? Might as well argue about something worthwhile.

No one knows your expressions, syntax or sense of humor as well as your spouse. Therefore, no one knows better than your spouse how well you're coming off — what works, what doesn't work, what should stay, what should go. What's too strong. What needs beefing up.

Your spouse loves you. He or she doesn't want you to sweat a presentation.

Rehearse In Front Of Any Group

It's impossible to assemble your audience before they are scheduled to hear you, so practice in front of any group you can get. Your co-workers, church, the P.T.A, even your kid's Scout troop.

A small committee, a regional sales force or a few members of the board of directors may not be your ultimate audience, but at least they provide a real rehearsal.

If it's an important occasion and it counts, so much the better. When the real day comes, it helps to know some of your audience and it helps to have some of your audience know you.

Dress Rehearsals Are A Myth

Dress rehearsals won't do the whole job. Just because you're dressed doesn't mean you're ready to present.

Being dressed is not enough! You'll need to rehearse a dress rehearsal before the final dress rehearsal.

By the time you get to the real dress rehearsal, everything should feel like you are in the actual presentation because dress rehearsals should duplicate the final event as closely as possible.

Rehearse In The Same Room

Get comfortable with everything before you have to. Get relaxed with everything from sizes and shapes to smells and sights. This is not only comforting, it's effective.

Rehearse In The Same Clothes

The same suit, the same dress, the same hat. Even the same shoes. You'll know ahead of time whether you look beautiful, handsome, cheap or flashy. You'll know if your clothes fit, whether you can move in them or whether they're too tight to let you relax?

You'll be able to make the appropriate changes before the audience cracks up.

Rehearse With All Your Mechanical Aids Before You Need Them

There's nothing worse than having a slide,

movie, or overhead projector quit in the middle of a key moment — unless it's devices that surprise you by not working at all.

Technophobia! We've all got it. Let's face it, sometimes it seems like technology and machines are out to get us. Presentation technology is no more reliable than home technology, except home tech only makes you mad, while presentation tech makes you look bad. It can trip you up, embarrass you, make you fail, make you sweat.

Rehearse In The Dark

Many presentations happen in dim or no light. So, why should you have to fiddle around and drop things on the big day? Why should you assume you can judge the audience, when you can't see them? Why practice facial and body expressions if they're going to be invisible?

Rehearsing in the same light you're going to

present in can answer these questions, and avoid all these pitfalls.

Doing it this way, you'll know if anybody can see a certain color, not to mention your whole outfit. You'll know if you can scratch an itch and get away with it. You'll know if you can tell whether or not they like how you're coming off. You'll know whether you have them in the palm of your hand or they have your neck between their hands.

Rehearse Behind A Podium

Is it too tall, too short, too fat or too thin? Is it steady? Does the light work? If so, is it too bright or too dim? Is the light aimed at your notes? Is there enough room for your notes?

Rehearsing behind the actual podium answers all these questions. The podium could surprise you by hiding your suit, revealing your suit, hiding your notes, blinding you or leaving you, and thus the audience, in the dark.

Not checking the podium in advance can end up making you very nervous and very sweaty.

Rehearse Hard-To-Pronounce Words

Most people don't know how to pronounce *plat de jour*, *hasta la vista*, *prosit* or *auf wiedersehen*. Not to mention Shalikashvili, Boutros-Boutros Ghali, or Schwarzenegger.

The only sin that's worse than mispronouncing someone's language is mispronouncing their name.

It's important to practice hard-to-pronounce words, names or anything in a foreign language.

You'll rarely write an order, sell a policy or initiate the uninitiated, if you mispronounce a native language or a family name.

Rehearse Jokes

As Laurence Olivier said, "Rhythm and timing are needed to create effects which must also appear to be spontaneous."

The secret of comedy is good timing.

"Take my wife . . . please," isn't very funny if you say, "Take my wife please."

Henny Youngman, Chevy Chase, George Carlin, John Belushi, Richard Prior and countless other comedians are great because they have impeccable timing. You may never be one of these geniuses, but you can benefit by rehearsing your timing.

Good timing is essential in any kind of public speaking from listing facts to giving a personal account. But jokes have two very precise goals: to be relevant and funny!

You'll need to know beforehand if they are

funny. Are they dirty, off-color or offensive instead of funny?

If they're dirty, clean them up. Nobody likes a person who tells a filthy joke. If they're off-color, correct the color. If they're bombs, drop them. A bad joke can blow any deal.

Jokes work harder if they're relevant. Telling an *apropos* joke can help make your point or just be relevant to your audience. And they help you make a good connection.

You get points for telling Army jokes to Army people. You'll lose points by telling an Army joke to Marines.

Picking a good, relevant joke, and then timing it well, is a hit instead of a miss.

Rehearsal Equals Casual

Rehearse to look casual even though you're not casual. Rehearse to sound casual even though you're not casual. If you do, you always sound off-the-cuff, even though you are never off-the-cuff.

There's no such thing as too much rehearsal. But no matter how often you rehearse, nothing's as good for your presentation skills as the real thing.

Never
Believe They're
Out To Get You

That's the most ridiculous idea I ever heard.
Groucho Marx

Most presenters know that friendly audiences are on their side. But most presenters don't know that hostile audiences are also on their side.

Neither audience is out to get you!

Friendly Audiences

Your own graduating class, your own branch of the service, your own branch of the company. Your co-workers, your fellow researchers, your fellow technicians. Believers in your cause, your church, your party, or your candidate. In other words, friendly audiences.

Ninety-nine percent of all audiences are friendly. And everybody knows friendly audiences are out to help you.

They want to hear your ideas. They want to be convinced. They're for your program. They laugh at your jokes. They're moved by your stories. They want to be converted. They want to be seduced. They're rooting for you to be good on your feet. They're always pulling for you. They're never pushing against you.

They're actually doing you a favor by being there, and letting you be there. Here are a few of the favors a friendly audience does for you:

They're building up you confidence.

They're giving you objective input. Without them, you are just talking to yourself. They're doing you a favor by giving your ideas a fresh hearing. All ideas get stale if they're just told to your own spouse. They need fresh air!

They're giving you a chance to show off your talent, humor and good looks. If you have any of these gifts, why not show them off?

If you think of friendly audiences as doing you a favor, they can't make you nervous.

Big Audiences

Just because it's a bigger audience doesn't mean they are hostile.

Big audiences aren't a threat, they're a gift.

The bigger the audience, the bigger the applause. The bigger the audience, the bigger the reaction. The bigger the laughs, cries, shock and amazement.

The bigger the audience, the more constructive criticism your ideas will receive. There are more of them out there, so the odds of hearing something constructive are better.

The bigger the audience, the more people who are out there pulling for you. More positive listeners equal more positive responses.

The bigger the audience, the bigger the favor you're going to get!

Hostile Audiences

Cut-throat companies, competing branches, other churches, the opposite party, supporters of the other cause or people who just want your job — it's hard to believe that hostile audiences like these can be on your side. But they can!

You're lucky to have hostile audiences. You just have to know how to use them. They provide you with the ultimate challenge: trial by fire.

If you can convince this group, you can convince any group. The hostile audiences that you will encounter are crammed with bullies and hecklers. Hecklers that try to throw you off. Bullies that try to embarrass you. Wise guys that try to make you nervous.

Bullies and hecklers at the Veteran's of Foreign Wars convention made President Clinton nervous when they razzed him about dodging the draft.

Network troublemakers were impatient with Vice-President Quayle when he blamed them for violent programming.

And bad comedians are often heckled off the stage.

Why not find a way to put these wise guys to good use?

For instance, why not treat bullies and hecklers like "hostile witnesses" are treated in court. Both prosecutors and defense attorneys use hostile witnesses to win cases. Why shouldn't you use a hostile audience to win cases, too?

Tips On Hostile Audiences

Hostile audiences take special preparation. But there are ways to use them to your advantage.

Tell Them You Don't Expect To Change Their Minds

They'll be relieved to hear you say changing their minds is not your job. And more relieved when you say, "Let's let history take care of changing your minds."

This will make you all more human, and diffuse any hostility your audience may be feeling.

You'll get a more receptive audience as a result. They'll be more ready to listen and be convinced.

Use Their Criticisms
To Bounce Off

Being criticized for a "bad" idea can help you think of another idea that will work better.

Being told that white deodorants are messy, can lead you to think of clear deodorants, which are not messy.

Being told that Halloween is the wrong day for an event, can lead you to think of using Guy Fawkes Day instead.

Use Their Arrogant Lines
As "Straight" Lines

There are no "straight men" like the ones you'll find in a hostile audience.

President Clinton used the Dole/Kemp hecklers as straight men. He quipped that if he had Dole and Kemp's record, he'd have to chant, too.

Johnny Carson, Jay Leno and David Letterman all use hecklers as straight men. In fact, hecklers often give these guys their next funny line.

Use Them To Help You Look Smart

A hostile client once made a presenter look smart in a TWA meeting.

"What a waste of money! How is anyone going to know that commercial was shot on the West Coast?" he jibed.

"The sun doesn't set over the ocean on the East Coast," was the answer.

Turn Hecklers' Chants Around
To Make Your Own Point

You can bounce off a "freedom now" chant to make your next point. Start with a compliment and let it lead you on: "Freedom now is a good point. Here's another good point . . ."

Use Hecklers To Give You
A Brand New Point

Look right at your most hostile listener and say, "Bill, you're right, this is a lousy idea. Maybe you can give us a better one."

Ask Them To Help You On Stage

When I was in the Army, drill sergeants used to make good use of the biggest trouble maker. The drill instructors would make them come up front and show the platoon what the wrong uniform looked like.

Convincing Them Is The
Best Medicine

You can't beat hostile audiences with force. You can't win by arguing, yelling or finger-pointing. But this doesn't mean they're not on your side.

You can put them on your team with reason,

common sense and sound logic. You can befriend them by convincing them.

It's impossible for them to argue against a point they have come to agree with.

They Sharpen Your Skills

Knives are smoothed and sharpened by rough stones. And presenters are smoothed and sharpened by rough audiences. Hostile audiences can provide a million opportunities to sharpen your presentation skills. The more hostile they are, the better you get as a presenter.

Nobody ever wants to present to a hostile audience. But they're not out to get you. If you use them right, they can help you.

Everybody knows friendly audiences do you a lot of favors because they're on your side. But if you know how to use a hostile audience — if you

Phil Slott

think positively about bullies, hecklers and big audiences — you'll find they aren't out to get you either.

Never
Be Snowed

Snow swept the world from end to end.
Boris Pasternak

The right-to-life and the right-to-choose. Professional sports and the Olympics. Apple and IBM. Pepsi and Coke. Gillette and Schick. The Travelers and Allstate. The Army and the Navy. McDonalds and Burger King. All have one thing in common. The snow job!

All organizations will snow you enough to lose your objectivity.

You can get snowed under from the outside. Or you can get snowed under from the inside.

Snowed From The Inside

Does your own organization make you believe its

propaganda, or do you want to believe it yourself?

Either way, you're snowed!

It's impossible to be critical of your *alma mater*.

It's impossible to be critical about your own company.

It's impossible to be objective about your own branch of the service, your own religion, your own hometown or state.

You can't be objective about solo sailing if your own yacht club has snowed you with the thrills of solo sailing.

Snowed From The Outside

It's hard but not impossible to be objective when your client is paying the bills.

It's hard to tell a razor company their razor's

too dull when they've already snowed you about how sharp it is.

It's hard to tell a pro-choice group that abortion should be a rare but occasional choice.

It's hard to tell a right-to-life group that abortion can save a life.

It's hard to tell an anti-smoking group that adult smokers have some rights. Or to tell a pro-smoking group that tobacco kills.

It's hard to tell an insurance company that its customers are worried about having their claims paid.

Whether from the inside or outside, organizations can seduce you until you join them in a kind of tunnel vision. But misguided loyalty is your downfall. As a result, you can no longer see the real problem or challenge.

Phil Slott

Getting snowed is the kiss of death for any presenter. You'll need your objectivity to present on the product, the competition or today's business environment.

The Product

You should never be snowed by the work ethic of state employees, the courage of Marines, the safety of cigarettes, the devotion of evangelical Christians, the comfort of a shave or the taste of a soft drink. You should never be seduced by the punctuality of an airline, the courtesy of a fast food-chain or the honesty of a bank.

These organizations want to snow you with their dreams, not be accurate about the truth.

The Competition

You could also become too snowed to present your analysis of the competition. Too snowed to present your point of view on whether the rivals are tougher, more dedicated or more efficient. That's because your client wants you to believe that its tougher, more determined and more cost-effective.

So, you're snowed! This means you can always be surprised. You and your client can be beaten out by a new offering or beaten to the punch with a quick copy.

Today's Environment

Is the mood of the country getting more conservative or more liberal? More devout? More straitlaced?

Do all Asians want to emigrate to America? Are people buying or renting more homes? Are families eating at home more often or eating out? Are they buying more or less insurance than ten years ago? Are teens high all the time, or straight most of the time? Is there, or isn't there, a glass ceiling?

If so, for whom? Women? Minorities? Liberal arts majors?

You can't pick the telling examples, choose the right music or present an accurate appraisal of these issues, if you're snowed.

If you're snowed, it's impossible to regain the necessary objectivity. It's impossible to overcome odds that are not in your favor.

How do you give a good presentation when you're snowed by your own organization? How do you give an objective presentation when you're snowed under the client that is paying the bills?

Reality Check

The best reality check is to check in with reality. Real sights, real sounds, real smells, reactions, feelings, real emotions. It's the real thing.

Have some real experiences.

Real danger. Real fear. Real courage. Real boredom. Real laughs. Real cries.

Talk to some real people. Real doctors, lawyers and Indian chiefs. Real tinkers, tailors, soldiers and spies.

Go to some real places. Monaco as well as Hoboken. Paris, Texas, as well as Paris, France. London and New London.

After a reality check, you can clear your thoughts with some research, even though research is second best. Even topnotch research is only an approximation of reality.

There's even a reality hierarchy in research. It ranges from trying to learn people's actual responses, to checking their biological responses as if they were laboratory rats.

One-on-one interviews are the closest technique to reality because they mean one person sitting down and interviewing another.

This is best because it often elicits a frank, intimate response that can be used meaningfully. The interviewer also sees the respondent's expressions and body language. Of course, you need a lot of interviews to make sure you have a large enough sample to be accurate.

Concept testing and focus groups are a little farther from reality, but at least they measure the overall idea.

Laboratory-rat testing is the farthest from reality. It may include a camera which monitors eye motion. Galvanic skin response which measures temperature, sweat and stress. And worst of all, Burke testing, which is a crude measure of gross memory without meaning.

Every organization whether you work within, or are hired as an outside contractor, will snow you and cause you to lose objectivity about the product or service and objectivity about the competition. Your best ally is an iron-clad reality check. And that means real reality, not clinical research, multiple choice or true and false questions.

Remember, reality beats research every time.

Phil Slott

Never
Forget Your Crutches

One must learn by doing the thing;
for though you think you know it,
you have no certainty until you try.
Sophocles

Unless you try a crutch yourself, you'll never be sure if it'll support your weight.

By crutches I mean presentation aids. All presenters need them. Props, slides, film, photographs, maps, charts, reports, music, audiotapes and literary quotes are all useful crutches. Even a hiding place called a podium is a useful crutch.

Nothing is worse than a crutch that doesn't work when it's supposed to, especially in the dark or when you're on stage and the focus of attention.

Symbols Are A Crutch

Alexander the Great, Adolph Hitler and Carl Sagan all understood this. Alexander the Great used himself. Hitler used folklore, and Carl Sagan used representations of life on Earth. The most useful crutch is a symbol.

Apple and Dell Computer both chose symbols as their presidents. Steve Jobs and Michael Dell were both founders of their companies and inspiring innovators in their teens and twenties. As presidents, they work very well because they are living symbols of both their consumers and companies. Much of the customer-base for these companies is in their teens and twenties. Even though Steve Jobs and Michael Dell are older now, they were symbols of youth at the outset, and the memory remains.

One of the most unusual crutches is attributed

to Fidel Castro — although he denies any part in choreographing the incident. During Castro's first speech to Cuba, from the steps of the recently overtaken Presidential Palace, a group of doves flew down from the palace walls and landed around Castro's feet. One landed on his shoulder and remained there while he spoke. The Biblical symbolism of the dove representing God's chosen one was not lost on the predominantly Catholic population. It was an interesting and intelligent use of symbolism. Even though Castro was an atheist, he understood the value of the symbol to his audience. Smart man.

The Audience Is A Crutch

You can use your audience as a crutch by asking for volunteers. They can help explain from their seats or help you explain onstage.

They can be an invaluable crutch for you when

you actually help them. If they ask questions, they put you in charge as you expand on a point to answer. If they ask for more information, they put you in command when you provide details, examples, definitions or show extra charts.

The audience can also provide a break from your planned text. They give an opportunity to *ad lib*, be spontaneous, relaxed, humorous and personal.

The king of using the audience as a crutch is Monty Hall of *Let's Make A Deal*, famous for saying to his of his audience, "Come on down."

By working with the audience, you can even make *their* agenda yours, by playing the moderator. This allows you to direct the audience back to the point of the presentation.

Reading Quotes Is A Crutch

Quotes take the heat off you. Let us face it:

people famous for their talent and brains say everything better than we can. Their ideas are better. Their syntax is better. Their philosophies are fully worked out.

For example, most people would rather hear the words of Gene Kelly, "If you look like you're working hard, you're not working hard enough," than hear a presenter say, "Working hard is a virtue." It may be mean the same, but it's less interesting.

Why not use the best people to help make your points? It adds sparkle and gives you a much-needed rest. You're less anxious because people immediately recognize the authority of Shakespeare or Churchill, and you get a break.

Scheduled Events Are Crutches

Presenters who schedule in reports from experts, reactions from the audience, and question-and-answer sessions, all get a break because they let someone else make their point.

The Volume Of Your Voice Is A Crutch

Many drill instructors know that changing the volume of the voice is an effective device. They know that whispering is more emphatic than shouting. That's why they often switch from shouting to whispering. The change in volume gets the platoon's attention.

Phil Dusenberry, BBDO's co-chairman, has used a quiet voice to his advantage for an entire career. He speaks quietly and his audience leans in to hear every word.

Measured Breathing Is A Crutch

Weight lifters pay a high price whenever they forget to breathe. So do presenters. Breathe deeply, normally and often while presenting.

If you make the mistake of holding your breath, you could cough, gag and have to gasp to catch your breath again. This will throw you off, and could make you look incompetent by ruining the magic of good timing.

Some of the best nuts-and-bolts crutches are listed above. But crutches can do, and be, a lot more than nuts-and-bolts for presenters.

Crutches Put You In Charge

Squealing speakers, ripped film, backwards slides, blurry overheads, misspelled words and missed cues can cost you control of the presentation.

These breakdowns can ruin a presentation that took months to prepare.

When the aids work smoothly, the presentation has a good shot at coming off as planned. Aids that work smoothly will mean that the audience reacts smoothly, and so will you.

Crutches Help You Communicate Better

Crutches improve your ability to communicate because they allow you to work with more than one of the five senses. They allow for making your point through touch, smell, taste, sound and vision. So, why not include fireworks for emphasis, or flowers for mood? The more sensory levels that you can communicate on, the better.

Crutches Keep You Organized

They are like following an outline. As you move from slide to slide, slide to film, film to tape, tape to chart, chart to map, map to globe, globe to ship, the next aid always reminds you of the next step. Crutches are great organizers.

Since you always know what's coming next,

you never panic or get lost. You have enough equanimity to underline important points, and you're calm enough to judge the audience reaction.

Crutches also serve as a breather for the presenter by diverting the audience's attention away from the speaker. Periodic breathers mean you won't lose your wind or your sense of order.

Crutches Keep You Calmer

Crutches will make for a calmer presenter. A calmer presenter is always a better presenter.

How do you make these hard-working crutches work even harder?

Practice Makes Perfect

Practice in the same venue, wear the same wardrobe, apply the same make-up, try the same lighting, props and materials, even check the same view from the same podium.

This may seem unnecessary, but trying the crutches beforehand, in a relaxed state of mind, means they won't surprise you.

A client of mine never practiced with the same slide projector he was going to use, and he was once mortified at a large sales meeting. He found the projector would only go forward and not back. And the buttons were so sensitive he found himself at one point fifteen slides ahead of his speech. Needless to say, he panicked and lost it!

You can avoid this by checking and rechecking all your crutches.

Be sure to choose the most appropriate crutches, bearing in mind the occasion, the situation, the audience, and most of all, your own comfort.

The Occasion

Some occasions call for the simplest "aw shucks,"

country-boy approach with plain mounted boards, iced tea and daisies all around. Others demand a slick, big-city feel with slides, martinis and roses.

A blackboard might be the right crutch for a college group, but it's the wrong crutch for an uptight business audience.

The Situation

Trying to win customers is a very different situation than quelling dissension in your own ranks. One situation needs a convincing product demonstration as a crutch. The other needs a no-holds-barred group discussion.

The Audience

Presenting to the Rotary Club requires completely different crutches than talking to Greenpeace.

Presenting to Generation X requires completely different crutches than presenting to the Silver Generation.

Knowing your audience is vital when it comes to choosing the right support.

But most important of all, you have to know where your own comfort lies. Some people are relaxed with white-on-black slides, others are relaxed using conventional overheads. Some people are happy behind a podium in the dark. Others want to stand in the audience and present from there.

There are many different styles and different crutches, but you're the only one who knows which ones will work for you.

Never
Run At The Mouth

We reached an agreement in broad,
but specific terms.
President Bill Clinton

Blah, blah, blah, blah. And one more thing: blah, blah and blah.

Running at the mouth means a presenter bores the audience by letting his mouth run on and on. It's only a matter of time until a bored audience becomes a dangerous audience, because bored always equals dangerous.

The first sign of a bored audience is when people sneak a peek at their watches, whisper to each other or perhaps check their lipstick.

Then comes the inevitable dangerous audience. Your listeners start disagreeing, asking too many questions, heckling and becoming sarcastic.

Finally, they'll say "no." No to more invest-ment, no to more insurance, no to another car, no to signing up. No to whatever it is you're asking for.

Running at the mouth does equal danger. It can ruin a career, flatten your business or squash your chances for advancement.

It's possible for a professor to be so boring that students drop his classes. For a salesman to be so boring that his last customer ruins his chances with his next. For a pastor to be so boring, the faithful lose heart. Or for a drill instructor to be so boring, his recruits won't re-enlist.

Acceptance speeches of all kinds are good examples of running at the mouth. These begin with Presidential acceptance speeches and go all the way to the Oscars and employee-of-the-year awards.

"Are you better-off today than you were four years ago?" "My program is what this country really needs." "Improved world trade is only part of what the voters say they want."

Presidential acceptance speeches are just one of the occasions that offer a chance to run at the mouth. People tend to bore audiences to death when they accept nominations for almost any office, at any level.

These occasions are sprinkled with platitudes about God, country and motherhood. The listeners are bored with generalizations about democracy, agriculture and crime. The audience's patience in tried with dissertations on defense, trade and economics.

Too bad, because these are all great chances to

say something meaningful and quickly get off stage.

Oscar acceptance speeches are classics! When it comes to running at the mouth everybody else is a bush-league amateur.

"I would like to thank my director, my producer, my writer, my cameraman, my hair stylist, and my make-up artist. Most of all, I want to thank my mother without whose help I wouldn't be standing here today."

But we don't have to go to Washington or Hollywood to find people who run at the mouth when they make speeches.

"It's a great honor to be chosen by my fellow employees of this fine company. It goes without saying that I know many of you could be up here instead of me. Probably one of you deserves this honor more than I do."

Phil Slott

The Essay Format

Instead of running at the mouth, use the time-honored essay format: "Tell them what you're going to tell them. Tell them. Then tell them what you told them."

Essayists have used it for centuries because three repetitions worked. Presenters should use it for the same reason.

Let's face it, most people are involved with their problems and their own lives. They need some repetition to cut through this internal dialogue.

You'll want to announce your point the first time. Then make your point a second time. And then reinforce the point for the third time. If you do all this, you'll be lucky if anybody remembers it anyway.

This is the only area where it's worth being

longwinded. You should *never* be longwinded for any other reason. You should be short-winded for every other reason.

Most of the time presenters should use as few words possible, not as many words as possible.

So, avoid long case histories about the product, the category, the marketplace, your family, friends or yourself.

The best discipline to ensure brevity is to reduce things to their essence. There's no discipline involved in inflating things to the breaking point.

For advertising presentations, I found shorter was always better. We often used to say, "when they say yes, zip up the bag and go home." Or "never talk your way out of a sale."

It's possible to kill your own sale. They have said yes, but you keep running at the mouth. You keep reinforcing the good reasons *why* they said yes. You keep rambling on until, pretty soon, you say something that makes them change their minds. Or you give them time to rethink the issue and reverse the decision.

We also used to remind ourselves that "short is better," "brief is effective," and "say it and sit down."

We learned these lessons the hard way. Dollars and cents, profit and loss, winning and losing taught us to say it fast and sit down!

Other ways of avoiding running at the mouth are staying centered, staying focused and staying organized.

Staying Centered

A central point will center you. You can't lose sight of a central point for it's never out of sight.

Having a central point is very calming. It's like having a home-base to return to, a hive to buzz around, or a campfire. A central point is like a life-ring to a presenter.

When you have a central point, you can always correct your direction if you get off course. You know as soon as you're digressing.

When you have a central point you can always recharge, gain new strength and start again.

Staying Focused

A focused point focuses you. It helps you avoid extraneous detail and the consequences of extraneous detail.

If you beat around the bush, the audience will shortly be confused, and they'll take that confusion out on you.

Staying Organized

An organized point organizes you. It's like trail markers that tell you where you are going.

Trail markers bring you back when you've lost the way. The markers will keep you from making the same point twice. Trail markers tell you what the next point is going to be.

Trail markers are acceptable crutches. They'll keep you from tripping up. They send the audience a signal that you have a plan.

The most important trail marker is an *outline*. Doing an outline organizes your thinking and makes your presentation better even as you actually create it. Later, having an outline keeps your presentation together while you give it.

Never give a presentation without doing an outline first. Then, be sure to use the outline while you speak.

The audience's attention is never given automatically. You have to earn it. Similarly, achieving a goal can never be taken for granted. You have to deserve that too.

If you want to deserve either, you can't run at the mouth.

Never
Be Too Positive

Accentuate the positive. Eliminate the negative.
Lyrics by Johnny Mercer and Harold Arlen

No matter what Mercer and Arlen's song says, it's just the opposite!

That advice may work for many occasions but it doesn't work for presentations. It's far more motivating to accentuate the negative and eliminate the positive.

The positive has become a big problem because it has a history of being *de rigueur* in presentations, whether given to students, the military, a sales force, trainees or even converts.

Everybody's afraid to be negative. It's as if God might strike a presenter dead if a negative word leaves his mouth.

Actually, the negative works harder than the positive.

It's more effective to tell people what they won't get than it is to tell them what they will get. This is exactly the opposite of conventional wisdom, and the opposite of instinctive behavior.

Experience has taught us to be consistently positive and avoid negativity at all costs. But in presentation, negativity is a friend and positivity is an enemy.

Accentuate The Negative

It's possible to be very positive by couching your point in negative terms.

I call this positive negativism.

For instance, "Never let 'em see you sweat" is a negative line in action. It was a well-received way of saying Dry Idea deodorant would keep you dry. It was well received by the client at the initial presentation and well received by consumers in the marketplace.

Lines like "Never let 'em see you sweat" work because what won't happen if you use Dry Idea (sweaty underarms) is more meaningful than what will happen if you do use Dry Idea (dry underarms).

A number of negative truths were behind this slogan. Truths like "yuppies don't like being out of control." Truths like "sweat is proof to yuppies that they are out of control."

We never said yuppies wanted to be dry because we knew they were more scared of being sweaty.

These negative truths led to a negative slogan, which was a good thing because the negative way of saying it was edgier.

Eliminate The Positive

Get rid of it! Positivity is goodie-two-shoes, syrupy pap! It's expected and therefore boring and ignorable. It's too New Age, which means it may be in vogue but it's been done too many times to be considered original.

It gets in the way of making an effective presentation.

Positivity really is our worst enemy.

"If you can't say anything nice, don't say anything at all." Sound advice, right? Wrong. It's often more meaningful to say the opposite. Sometimes it's necessary to say, "Don't do that."

If you'd only said that, you might have avoided a disaster!

"Mmmm, mmmm, good!" "Be all that you can be." Good slogans, right? Not really. They could have worked harder.

Campbell's just changed its slogan from "Mmmm, mmmm good," to "Nothing is mmmm, mmmm better." This slogan sets up a competitive claim using the word "nothing," and as a result, soup sales are back on the rise.

And the Army should have told young people what can be avoided by joining the Army, instead of asking them to try to realize some mythical potential. Most recruits are from the inner city and have faced drugs, crime, pregnancy or unemployment before their teens. They need to be promised they can miss all that. Something that adds up to: "Don't be all you might be."

Again, by being negative, there's an opportunity for more convincing commercials with the certainty of more recruits for the Army.

When the new advertising campaigns for Campbell's and the Army were originally presented, the presenters probably made the typical mistake of accentuating the positive and eliminating the negative, because these slogans are not even close to being edgy enough. Especially in the case of the Army, the concept was out of touch with the audience.

A great many people are critical, negative, cynical and sarcastic. So, if you're never negative, or always positive, it's unlikely you'll be on the same wavelength as your audience.

Let's compare some positive and some negative presentation versions:

Bonds

A. Bonds are safe enough for you.

B. Bonds are too safe for you.

They both say bonds are safe. But the negative

presentation works better. It makes people insist on buying bonds. It's called a negative sell.

Cars

A. This car performs perfectly for your needs; you should buy it.

B. This car may be too powerful for you. You shouldn't even touch it!

Negative sell again.

There aren't many guys, who have the money to buy, who'll turn down a car that's "too powerful."

Promotions

A. Good luck getting the next job.

B. I hope you never get the next job. It's nothing but headaches!

Who wouldn't want the next job after they

hear it's nothing but headaches? After all, aren't job headaches a status symbol everybody wants to have?

Horses

My brother raises Icelandic horses for a living.

To advertise them, he originally wanted to say positive things such as, they are a great riding experience, they have five different gaits, Icelandic horses are the original ancient horse.

This is all true and meaningful to an expert customer, but none of it is very motivating to the uninitiated rider.

I convinced him to present a more meaningful negative version in the headline: "Icelandic horses may not be for you."

Now he uses the story about smoothness and ancient gaits in the body copy of his brochure.

Phil Slott   **153**

"Icelandic Horses may not be for you" is a tough thing for him to lead with. After all, he breeds them, mucks out the stalls and he's the owner. Leading with the negative sell resulted in more requests for information, and ultimately, more sales.

The negative sell is the best sell, but it's a scary sell.

The Marines

"We're looking for a few good men" is a great example of a negative sell at work. And it does work. The Marine Corps always has enough recruits. At times they've had too many.

That's because nobody wants to be one of many good men, but many want to be one of "the Few, the Proud, the Marines."

This is the perfect example of being positive by being meaningfully negative.

Smoking / Drugs

Obviously, quitting smoking and not doing drugs are good things to accomplish.

The anti-tobacco people could have said you'll feel good if you don't smoke. The anti-drug cause could have said you'll feel good if you don't take drugs.

But the anti-smoking lobby decided to say, "Don't smoke," and the anti-drug lobby decided to say, "Just say no."

Both causes chose the negative way of expressing their messages because it's more convincing.

"Accentuate the positive and eliminate the negative" worked in the old song, but in practice

I've found it's just the opposite in crafting a presentation. Communicating negatively is more unusual and, therefore, more effective than communicating positively.

Positive negativism is the presenter's best friend.

Never
Get Caught Lying

One lie will destroy a whole reputation for integrity.
Baltasar Gracian

Everybody lies occasionally, but lying during a presentation means a lot more than not telling the truth.

There's a whole hierarchy of lies that starts with simply omitting the truth, and goes all the way to harmful untruths.

Let's start with the least offensive mode that many presenters use. It's euphemistically called a sin of omission.

Sin Of Omission

A sin of omission is as good as a lie. That's why it's called a sin.

One very newsworthy example is the overzealous investment salesman who never mentions how risky derivative investments are.

Examples from the world of advertising abound. Like not telling a client that a commercial the client loves will cost a lot to produce.

Everybody wants to be the bearer of good tidings, but nobody wants to be the bearer of bad tidings.

In the oath "the truth, the whole truth, and nothing but the truth," the keys words are the whole truth. The whole truth usually includes some bad news. That's why a partial truth is a sin of omission.

Most people tell the truth in court but few people do it in presentations. However, being found guilty and punished is guaranteed in both cases. As we will see, the punishment fits the crime, in presentations too. But first, here are more euphemisms for lies. They get worse and worse.

Coloring The Truth

Coloring the truth is a standard technique used by too many presenters. Coloring the truth may seem harmless, but color counts! A different color can give the audience a false impression.

When you have to color the truth, it must mean you didn't like the original color. You've decided that colored truth works better than plain truth.

The influence of New-Agers has created a style of presentation that demands coloring the truth. They absolutely insist on being positive about everything, whether it's called for or not.

So, they color the truth from "sales are down and we need to rethink our strategy" to "this company is doing the best it can." They color the truth from "this soft drink tastes lousy" to "this soft drink tastes better than it used to." And they color the truth from "that commercial stinks" to "that commercial is very interesting."

These expressions give a false impression.

At this point coloring the truth has become a deplorable New Age habit that seeps into presentation style. Coloring the truth is far from being a minor change. When it happens, the real truth is disguised and a wrong course of action could result.

Changing Your Mind

We all change our minds once in a while, right? Sure, but the problem for presenters is that this natural process will cause you to lose credibility in a presentation venue.

Feel free to change your mind before a presentation and never change it in the middle of a presentation.

An indecisive thinking process may be a natural thing in private but it can play havoc in a public setting. Make up your mind what you are going to say and stick to it. The moment of presentation is no time to think things over.

Polite Lies

Polite lies are the mildest kind, and presenters tell them quite often.

They make themselves feel better about doing it because they do it politely. They'll smile and say thanks, while they're lying.

Then they excuse themselves by telling themselves it was the thing to do and didn't hurt anyone.

Phil Slott   **161**

But a polite lie can be as bad, or worse, than an impolite lie.

"I'd like to join you, but I'm tied up" is no better than "I don't want to join you." These days everybody speaks in code and, everybody also knows how to decipher code.

Dreamy Lies

We all fantasize. We're all wishful thinkers on occasion. We all revise history to suit the present. Most of the time this not only sounds like a good dream, it is a good dream.

But in presentations, fantasies had better match reality, wishes had better come true, and history had better match the past. What comes off as positive thinking in everyday life can come off as misrepresentation in a presentation.

Be careful of fantasy! The audience wants facts

that they can bank on, not dreams they can sleep on. They want real goals and challenges. They want to know exactly what peaks they have to climb, and exactly what valleys they might encounter.

If they catch you dreaming, it'll be a bad dream for sure.

Exaggerating

Every organization, from a company in business to an infantry company, tries to instill pride and *esprit de corps* in its members.

A natural result of this is to seek to please people by stretching the truth, to make points by exaggerating. To apple polish by maximizing good results and kiss ass by minimizing negative results.

Lying of this sort is now considered a laudable

skill in many organizations. Therefore it has become fairly standard in presentations. You know you can get ahead the same way everybody else does.

Minimizing or maximizing means you're willing to adjust dates, numbers and times. You're willing to make the change, if it puts you or the client in a favorable light.

But exaggeration can also discredit you for being wrong. Reality will challenge, try and test exaggerations, and can lead to embarrassment and failure.

Bald-Faced Lying

Now for the most worst kind of lie — bald-faced lying.

To exaggerate may be more about courting

favor than anything else, but a bald-faced lie is morally wrong.

Bald-faced lying means someone has decided to tell a downright untruth for reasons of his own. He has decided that profit, winning, a promotion or self-aggrandizement are more important than morality.

He's decided that getting ahead is more important than doing the right thing. And while getting ahead may be more important, you should never get caught lying in a presentation.

Once the audience recognizes you as a liar, they'll want you to slip up, fail and be embarrassed. They'll want to see you sweat.

This could start with an observations like: "Gee Ed, my data doesn't match yours." And could end with punishment of ridicule, or in Groucho's phrase, "That's the most ridiculous thing I ever heard!"

Lying ruins credibility. And once you're known as a liar, they audience will not believe a word you say.

Further, one lie usually leads to another, and before you know it, you're stuck with a tar baby.

Getting caught lying leads to blowing it. And blowing it leads to sweating it.

You'll have the same reaction you did when your parents called you on the carpet, only now an audience is calling you out.

Truth snowballs just as lying snowballs. When it does, you become known as a trustworthy person. People end up believing every word from start to finish. This means an audience will agree or a client will sign on the bottom line.

Never
Be Arrogant

*Feed, arrogance and supple knees
are the proud man's fees.*
William Shakespeare

The dictionary defines arrogance as "the act or quality of having unwarranted pride and self importance." Dictionary synonyms include haughtiness, presumption, self conceit, as well as vanity.

My synonyms include schmuck, egotist, show-boat, grandstander, hot-dog and wise guy.

Arrogant people aren't in touch with their own humanity or that of the audience. Being so far out of the human loop makes these guys domineering and abrupt.

Possibly, they feel inferior so they act superior. They'll rush to present unproved results. They aren't clear because they aren't willing to explain.

Wise guys like this care more about what they're going to say next than they do about what the audience wants to hear.

But nothing blows a deal like gloating over it, and most audiences dislike a braggart. If you begin this way, the audience will be out to get you the rest of the time.

They won't want to buy your storm windows, join your executive team, vote for your candidate or give you the account.

Sometimes when presenters feel threatened by an audience, they will puff out their chests and act defensively. A number of presenters are even willing to threaten their listeners. We've all heard these: "Try to pay attention!" A plea from a frustrated boss. "This will be on the test." The nagging reminder of a worried professor. "If I can do it, you can do it." A threat from a sports coach. "If you don't listen up, you'll never complete the mission!" A drill instructor's classic.

Arrogant presenting such as this declares war on the audience. In return, the audience wants the boss to falter or wants the professor to be in the wrong. The troops now can't wait for the drill instructor to make mistakes.

It's a natural reaction to want to turn wise guys into dumb guys.

One recent example of arrogant behavior is the state supreme court judge who posted the Ten Commandments prominently in his courtroom. Nothing's wrong with the Ten Commandments. But the US Constitution calls for a separation of church and state.

That Judge is paid by government, yet he's in effect saying there's no separation of church and state in his courtroom. Will his opinions and decisions reflect the law, or has he placed his personal beliefs above the law?

An example of a situation where arrogance could have been used, but wasn't, is "The Power of Prayer," the name of a recent study whose findings prove that prayer works. The study shows that prayer can be helpful medically.

It's now scientifically certain that prayer and spiritual belief can speed the recovery process. Patients who pray actually get better faster!

The power of prayer has always been a trusted home remedy, but now it's recognized as a medical remedy. This promising scientific finding would never be believed if it had been presented arrogantly.

On the other hand, arrogance has occasionally made respected scientists rush to judgment.

Scientists can drive many of us crazy by plodding along too methodically. They typically insist on proving test results over and over. "It works *in vitro*, but will it work *in vivo*?" It seems they take forever to bring their findings out of the test tube and into the street.

But the announcement about cold fusion several years ago was a case where arrogance preceded the proper scientific certainty because it preceded proper scientific method.

The promise of cold fusion got physicists so excited, they got arrogant. So arrogant, they wrongly presented cold fusion as a safe replacement for nuclear fusion before it was established as a reality.

If there ever was a case where arrogance hurt a presentation, this was it.

Arrogance can hurt political presentations too.

Phil Slott   171

People are familiar with the arrogance of Newt Gingrich. But the fact is, here there's arrogance on either side. The same could be said of Richard Gephardt as of Newt Gingrich.

These are both smart and caring politicians. But, like John Sununu before them, they're both victims of arrogance.

And, like John Sununu, before them, their solid points of view are often ignored, rebuked or scoffed at.

Successful presentations trade arrogance for humility.

Humility

The dictionary defines humility as "the absence of pride or self-assertion."

My definition includes modesty, listening and politeness.

This sounds like treacly eyewash or self-righteous pap. But, it's possible to be humble and have a cool attitude at the same time. In fact, cool people are often humble.

Acts of humility include statements like "That's a very good question!" "I'm glad you made that point." "Thank you for making us aware of that."

Humility in action also includes giving credit for other people's ideas, giving away ownership, giving compliments, giving explanations, giving thanks, reacting to humor with generosity, keeping put-downs to yourself and getting off "send."

Give Credit

People are proud of their ideas and their ownership. They're also painfully sensitive when someone tries to steal them. Why should you step on their toes by taking credit for an idea that's not yours? Don't even try.

Giving credit makes friends, makes the point and it's always appreciated. If you don't give credit, where credit is due, you're asking for a revolt.

Give Compliments

Here's a chance to take your role as featured speaker and turn it around.

Suddenly instead of people being impressed with you, and hanging on your every word, you're impressed with them, and hanging on their every word.

Give Rare Explanations

Correct yourself when you misspeak or make a mistake.

Say "there's no excuse for being late." "I'm supposed to know how to work this thing." Or, "I know this slide is too small to see in the back row."

Give Thanks

Thank participants if they make a good point, ask an excellent question, reveal inside info or clarify.

Thank volunteers for helping you do demonstrations and thank the whole audience for listening. Which they will, if you're polite.

Good manners is good presenting.

Give Humor Generously

Humor should be your gift to members of the audience. Be self-deprecating with a chuckle.

Say things like: "I never liked this tie either." "I can't even read my own handwriting." Or, "Does anybody here know how to work this podium light?"

If you're humble and generous with your jokes, they'll relax, listen better and like you better.

Hold The Put-Downs

Don't put others down.

Being in charge can inflate the ego. You're the center of attention, the resident expert and the star of the show, all rolled into one.

From this heightened position, it's easy to become arrogant and put people down. Don't. Putting people down will compromise the overall effectiveness of your presentation. It will make the audience defensive, interfere with their attention span, cause restlessness, cause heckling and ultimately can make sure you don't get the order.

Get Off "Send"

Don't be so full of yourself, you can't tell how anybody's reacting. If you'd get off send and get on receive once in a while, you could learn something.

If you do, you'll be more popular.

We all expect authority figures to be self-centered, so it's surprisingly lovable when they're not.

Arrogance is a common defense mechanism among presenters, because presenters often feel threatened. They feel inferior, so they act superior, by gloating.

The cure for the sin of arrogance is the virtue of humility.

It is possible to be humble and cool at once.

Phil Slott   **177**

Never
Be Too Serious

" How many New Yorkers does it take to put in a light bulb?"

"One, but he's on break."

See, now you're listening.

Actors, professors, toastmasters and salesmen have always known the virtue of starting with a joke. They know that a joke gets the audience's attention.

Because humor equals shock. Humor makes an audience more receptive by loosening people up.

As a result, the presentation itself becomes more personal. Presentations are more successful when your relationship with the audience is one-on-one.

Humor can be hard-working and do a lot of important jobs.

Humor Can Make The Point

Being funny does more than make presentations personal. It has tangible effects, it can help convince and it can reinforce your goals.

Humor is most effective when the joke or crack is relevant. A joke about confusion can help you make a point about restructuring the organization. A joke about poor service can help you make your point about good service. A joke about neatness says something about sloppiness.

And jokes can certainly underscore or defeat a point. Nothing makes something look as bad as making it look silly with a joke.

Humor Can Help Make It Your Agenda

Telling jokes helps bring any presentation back to your agenda because it puts you in charge.

The audience does your bidding by laughing at your jokes — when you want them to.

Humor Relaxes Your Audience

Starting with a joke is good, but continuing to be loose and light is better. Pepper your whole part with humor.

There's no way an audience can be relaxed and receptive the whole time if you only tell them one joke.

Humor Makes You Likable

People are more likely to buy a program, a product or a point of view from someone they like. They warm to funny people.

Jokes can help you ask for an order — and

every presentation asks for some kind of order. The presentation asks if they'll buy this car, agree to this financial plan, strive for this goal, embrace this philosophy or vote for this candidate.

So give your joke the funny test. If it fails, it could mean a lot more than a joke bombing and people not laughing.

Jokes do work, but we are not all born funny. Suppose you never hear any jokes or remember them? Suppose you forget the punch line? This calls for learning some all-purpose joke and some specific jokes.

The All-Purpose Joke

If you can't think of something more spontaneous, use the all-purpose joke. It's a joke that fits any time, any place with any group — a joke you have in reserve. For example:

"I wanted to talk to you today, but I seem to have forgotten my notes."

Or "I wish I was smart enough to work this podium light."

Or, "I'll stand behind this podium, because I don't want you to see this dress doesn't go with these shoes." (This works best for a man.)

Specific Jokes

Specific jokes as a rule are funnier. The more specific they are to your audience, the funnier they are. It's worth making a joke specific to a big city, if you're in one or a rural area if you're in the country. Make jokes specific to those you're addressing.

It's worth it to tell the specific jokes, but make sure you pick the right sports joke, state joke or pertinent career joke. If you pick the wrong specific joke, you'll end up with egg on your face.

Also, whatever you do, stay away from sex, race, politics and religion. Even if you handle these topics well, a joke will offend someone. There's a good reason why they say "never talk politics or religion."

How about these specific jokes:

For New York City

Visitor: Can you tell me where the Empire State Building is or should I just go to hell?

For A Small Town

My town is so small, all the ladies had the same dress on at the Easter Parade.

For California

How many Californians does it take to change a light bulb?

Ten. One to change the lightbulb, and nine to share the experience.

For The Marines

Is it true all the food in the Marine Corps gives your jaw a hard workout?

For Kids

I know a great "knock, knock" joke. You start it off.

Specific jokes work especially well if you choose the appropriate ones for the audience. But suppose your humor bombs?

Using humor can be risky because it can backfire. Members of the audience can sit on their hands, roll their eyes and sigh instead of laughing uproariously. You'll need to know how to react and continue.

Make a joke out of the fact that they are not laughing. Like, "Guess it was better when

Groucho said it." This allows you to recoup and continue in a light-hearted way.

First-time presenters should be cautious with their use of humor. There's no reason to make yourself sweat if you don't have to.

Humor has not only worked for me as a presenter, but on me as a prospective buyer.

I remember when my real estate agent was funny and said: "They're gonna bury me here," instead of being boring and saying, "I like it here in Hawaii."

Partly as a result of what his joke conveyed, I bought twelve remote acres, 3,000 miles from the US mainland. And I've since bought twelve more acres from him.

Proof positive — his humor worked!

Never forget that people come to presentations for entertainment. They can get information from books, computers, movies and magazines. People never attend a presentation just for the facts.

They really come to see you in action. Maybe they've heard you're good on your feet. Maybe they've heard listening to you is worth their time. Maybe they think your showmanship is a welcome break from doing hard work in the office.

Think about it: a presentation is frequently the most fun working people have at their jobs. A glimmer of light in a sea of darkness.

Props, jokes, stories, acting — what a great way to get the necessary scoop.

We can't all be naturals. People excuse themselves for being corny by saying, "Sorry, I've never had a good sense of humor."

But not having a good sense of humor or a natural sense of humor is no longer an excuse for not being funny. There are thousands of new jokes written for daytime talk shows, late-night talk shows, variety shows, drive-time shows, magazine cartoons, joke books, even the daily comics.

There's never a reason you can't tell jokes because we can all tell someone else's jokes.

There's no reason we should have to write our own material. Often, even comedians don't write their own stuff.

Professional comedy writers write funny jokes everyday. So why not use the best jokes in the business?

Being deadly serious will compromise any presentation, but being funny will help it.

Humor helps make the point, helps you control the agenda and makes you likable.

Phil Slott

Specific jokes are always better than an all-purpose joke even though an all-purpose joke can come in handy.

Remember, the folks come to be entertained, not lectured. And there's no reason not to use the best jokes you can whether you write them or not.

Never
Stop Acting

The leader of men must be an actor.
General George Patton

If you don't act well, you won't present well. Presenters who are not natural actors would be advised to take standard acting lessons. They should learn acting basics. Like learning how to keep silent, how to stay completely still and how to use emotion for maximum effect.

An actor aims at a desired result from a role.

In the theater, the goal is entertainment.

In undercover police work, the goal is to pose as a criminal.

In presentations, the goal of acting is equally practical.

So, wheedle them, impress them, amuse them,

Phil Slott   **189**

sadden them, frighten them, anger them, excite them or calm them.

Whether you're on a theatre stage or in a conference room, whether you're on the boards or on the company board, acting is required.

If you want them to laugh, cry or carefully weigh a decision or if you're a presenter in journalism, advertising, sales, medicine or science, you'll learn to accept the necessity of acting.

Whenever you present, you're in show business.

A presentation is no time to bore an audience with the real you. Presentations are the wrong format to discuss your neuroses, your time in the military or any problems you may have at home.

Presentations are an opportunity to enthrall the audience with the best in you.

The role of emotion in presentations could take a page out of an actor's notebook.

Like emotion in acting, emotion in presentations is best based on real-life. As any actor knows, a performance is more believable if it's based on actual experience.

As one real-life example from advertising, a father used his son's words to present a television story board for the Ideal Toy account. They bought it.

You can base a presentation on your own life by harking back to a similar situation. Hark back to what you said and how you felt, then use the former occasion to make the current occasion more believable.

Emotion is always useful, but you should always be unemotional about its use. To be objective and choose the right emotion for the job at hand makes dollars-and-cents sense.

It can cost time, money or goodwill to become too emotional. Emotions can run away with you, or you might pick the wrong emotion.

Presenters should rehearse as actors, look and act like actors. After all, they are actors!

Whatever business you're in, it helps to think of yourself as a member of a cast with a performance to stage.

You could play one of many personal roles, or it could be one of many business roles.

If none of the roles below are the real you — ACT! If you don't believe any of the roles below — act!

Why let reality cause failure when you can act.

Here are some roles you can act out.

The Teammate

No matter who you're presenting to, team spirit is the price of entry. The audience wants to know they can count on you, that their problems are your problems and that you're all in this together.

Your role is to appear to put the uniform on and join the squad. Your role is to act like a member of the team

The Worrier

If you're presenting as an employee of your own company, your worry is expected. If you're presenting as a guest, your worry is hoped for.

So assume the role. Look worried, walk worried, dress worried, seem worried, act worried!

The Square

One competition that's inherently present in every organization is "who's-the-squarest."

You as a presenter can act and win this contest. You'll have to act like the squarest one there even if the room is full of squares. Why? Because squares are universally trusted.

If you're really cool and not square, act square!

Ms. Optimistic

Many organizations are counting on a presenter to have the optimism they don't have anymore. People have lost their enthusiasm over time. You're expected to bring it back.

Therefore optimism is your ticket to ride. It's your ticket to presenting.

You'll want to be more optimistic about increasing sales, becoming number one, getting federal approval, being awarded a patent or winning an Academy Award.

If you don't believe any of these things will happen, act as if you do.

Faked optimism is better than real pessimism.

Mr. Concerned

In this situation as a presenter, I care more about quality, more about the guarantee, more about justice, more about Old Glory, more about risk and reward, more about trade-offs, more about the school's reputation, more about expanding internationally, more about the sharpness of the blade, more about the salt content, more about the secrecy of the formula, more about the headache sufferer's pain, more about customer complaints — I care more than you do!

It's important to act like you care more than the client. Whoever hired you has lost concern over time, just as he lost enthusiasm. You're paid to care in the present.

If you don't care, act like you care! Faked concern is better than real indifference.

Phil Slott   195

The Tough Guy

Tough. Isn't that a male word? Doesn't that mean *macho*? Isn't that exclusive to Marines, jock-strappers and steelworkers?

Used to be. But these days, tough is unisex. It applies equally to both genders. Both genders now act tough on athletic teams, in foxholes and at various jobs in the workplace.

Most presenters don't feel tough when they present, but they can act tough.

Tough has come to mean focusing on the big picture, not sweating the details. Tough means keeping your end up, not complaining and being off-handed about what's important.

If you're not feeling tough, it just means you need to act tough. Acting tough is better than being a wimp.

The goals of method acting may be more serious than yours, but you as a presenter have a lot to learn from the theater. You'll only present as well as you act.

Presentation and the theater are both based in your experience. Both are based in show biz. Both are based on emotion and both require you to rehearse.

But there was one time, at least, when I didn't have to act, as a presenter, because my feelings were real. When I delivered my good-bye speech after twenty-six years in advertising, ninety percent of those in the audience were strangers. I used the occasion to tell five hundred people about the word *aloha*, with real emotion.

I looked out in the audience and said, "*Aloha* means three things. *Aloha* means hello. *Aloha* means good-bye. *Aloha* means I love you."

Phil Slott   **197**

Because I understood the importance of performing in presentations, I was able to use "I love you" as my last three words in the field of advertising.

Never
Say Never

"I'll never think of a good point."

"They'll never remember anything."

"This stuff will never work."

"I'll never be able to face all those people."

Talk like this is a recipe for disaster! But you can break this habit.

Think about crossing the stage to accept an Oscar. Imagine you're climbing the pedestal to get a gold medal. Think about where to hang a Pulitzer prize in your office.

In short, they'll never see you sweat if you never say never.

Phil Slott   **199**

Instead you can say, "I'm the best presenter in the company." "Nobody presents this material better than I do." "I'm gonna sell a million of these things."

Good! That's more like it!

Now you have the confidence of a real showman. And the more you present, the more confident you'll be. Unlike my early days, you'll never have to pray, before a presentation again.